Open with God

Open with God

Prayers for meetings through the year

Christine Odell

British Library Cataloguing in Publication data

A catalogue record for this book is available
from the British Library

ISBN 1 85852 262 5

First published by Inspire
4 John Wesley Road
Werrington
Peterborough PE4 6ZP

Printed and bound in Great Britain by
Stanley L Hunt Printers, Rushden

Dedication

This book is lovingly dedicated to my parents
Alan and Averil Odell
who encourage me to see
with both heart and mind.

Foreword

This book is far more than a series of prayers for use at church meetings – it is a treasure-chest of material that will be useful in an enormous variety of contexts and situations. Christine Odell challenges us to open up to God some of the most sensitive, beautiful and difficult aspects of our human experience.

The primary aim of the book is to provide prayer-resources for meetings. Meetings are fascinating and complicated things. People come with a whole range of expectations and hidden agendas, and church gatherings have the additional ingredients of faith and fellowship, beliefs passionately held, and divisions often acutely painful. Whether we are attending a church business meeting or a Bible-study, a speaker meeting or a planning group, the person responsible for the prayers has an important task. Minds and hearts need to be quietened and focused on the reason for the gathering. We need to be sensitive to the other people present. And, most of all, we need to place whatever we are doing in the wider context of our calling to be bearers of Christ's love in the world.

Christine's Prayers for Various Occasions addresses all these needs, ranging from *Prayers for Guidance* to suggestions for that tricky area of *Fundraising*. Her material also takes us, rightly, into issues of *Outreach* and *The World Church*. The style and content of her prayers helps us avoid the notion that prayers are just a tiresome duty, to be tacked on to the beginning or end of a meeting and 'got through' as quickly as possible. There is grit and a sense of challenge in this collection, and painful issues are not dodged. To give one example, *Times of Crisis II* addresses those times when a congregation is torn apart by conflict and bitterness, and this section, like many others in the book, could fruitfully be reproduced on service sheets or notices for people to pray with during the week.

But there is more. Those responsible for leading praying at all kinds of events will breathe a sigh of relief at having ideas for occasions such as a *Flower Festival*, as well as sensitive material for a *Farewell* to a friend, or a *Death* of someone known to the group, or a national *Disaster*. Prayers at the time of *Divorce* are particularly striking and will fulfil an important pastoral need.

The Calendar of Prayers will enrich our journey through the rhythms and imagery of the seasons in the church's year. Interwoven with this, the days concerned with educational, social and world issues come as a welcome reminder that faith is concerned with all of life. This section of the book could be used as a helpful manual for personal prayer as well as a resource for groups and gatherings.

Christine's suggestions for visual elements and symbolic actions open up all sorts of imaginative and creative possibilities. As they also include suggested Bible passages, many of Christine's prayers are in fact short liturgies, and could easily be adapted for use in public worship. In addition, many of them lend themselves to use at house meetings (not just the one entitled *House Groups*).

My only anxiety about the book is that its contents might be under-used! It would be sad if, for example, the excellent prayers about *Drama* were only used on the rare occasion of a local play performance, or the prayers for *Racial Justice* only used in September. I hope that readers will use Christine's prayers in all sorts of situations, in order to do justice to the breadth of vision with which this book was written.

Angela Ashwin
Writer and lecturer on spirituality

Contents

Introduction

Some people can talk about anything off the top of their heads. Some find it much harder to express their thoughts in a clear and truthful way and would rather prepare and write them down.

All we need to pray is to be 'open with God'. We do not need anything written down. We do not always need words themselves. But many of us find leading other people in prayer a daunting responsibility and look for help with finding words through which God's Spirit can assist us to pray together.

These prayers have been written to be used by those who have been called upon to lead opening worship at a weekday meeting and who are looking for help. Although the prayers could be used in Sunday worship, most of them do not fit into one of the categories of prayer included in the liturgy. Instead, they are intended for use on occasions where there may be only one main prayer. The first part of the book contains a calendar of prayers written for specific dates during the Church year or for special times designated as dates to remember the needs of different groups of people. The second part contains prayers written for occasions and occurrences in the life of the church congregation or in the news; these are in alphabetical order. All the prayers are listed in the index.

When you use this book, please do not just pick it up and read out a prayer. Every prayer to share needs to be prepared prayerfully. There are spaces left in some of the prayers, so that they can be 'personalised' to the needs and concerns of the meeting, community or of the moment. Some prayers contain responses that need to be learnt by those present at the outset or shared in written form, and there are times of silence of which they may need to be forewarned. Most of them need a closing sentence and an 'Amen' adding at the end. Those using these prayers should feel free to adapt or change them whenever this is desirable or necessary.

I am sometimes asked, 'How do you go about writing your prayers?' The honest answer is that I do not know. But I am acutely aware of the presence of the Spirit in the making of them, mingling with what is in my head and heart and persuading words out of my pencil. Creativity, and especially that guided by the Spirit, is an ongoing process – so please use these prayers creatively!

There are many people from among my family, friends and church families whom I would like to thank for their support and interest while I was writing this book, but my special thanks go to:

Peter Sheasby, my husband, without whose love, help, support and ministerial stipend my writing would not be possible;

Anna, our terrific teenager;

Natalie Watson, my editor at Inspire, who has been a real 'daughter of encouragement', for all her help and guidance.

Thanks are also due to the West Yorkshire District of the Methodist Church for agreeing to the use of the title *Open with God* which has been used for one of their WYS prayer booklets.

Fear not to enter his courts in the slenderness
Of the poor wealth thou wouldst reckon as
thine;
Truth in its beauty, and love in its tenderness,
These are the offerings to lay on his shrine.

John Samuel Bewley Monsell

Christine Odell
October 2004

Calendar of Prayers

JANUARY – New Year
Reading: Revelation 21.1-7

'And the one who was seated on the throne said,
"See, I am making all things new."'

Sometimes, God of the present moment,
we feel afraid of things that are new.
Life changes around us so quickly
that we struggle to keep up.
Some changes we can see are good
but others leave us longing for the past.
We need the help of your Spirit
to see where you are in this present age
and to direct our footsteps down new paths.

L: God who makes all things new:
R: Renew and bless us.

We need to be made new, saving God,
because your world is weary of old ways,
of warfare, injustice, poverty and selfishness.
We pray for its leaders, for ....
Paint for us a picture of your new earth
so we can recognise your handiwork in the world
and support and follow and help
those seeking to do your new things.

L: God who makes all things new:
R: Renew and bless us.

We look for your newness in our lives;
we are tired of our failure to love and understand,
our failure to make our lives worthy of you.
We are tired of the things that hold our loving back,
our fear, our ignorance, our lack of vision.

We pray for all whose lives are frustrated
by illness, loss and limitations, for ....

L: God who makes all things new:
R: Renew and bless us.

God of this new year, we pray for the days to come.
We have heard your offer to make us new
if we will put our trust in the saving love of Jesus.
With your help we will open our hearts and minds
to take into our lives the power
        of your transforming Spirit.

JANUARY – Covenant

Reading: Jeremiah 31.31-34

Loving God, help us to understand
what it means for us to say that
'You are our God
and we are your people.'

'You are our God.'
You are everything to us.
You give us all we need.
If we build our lives on you
and your loving promises
we shall have life in all its fullness.
But we confess, forgiving Parent,
we often forget to put you first
to be open and trusting with you.
This new year, help us to make a fresh start
and keep our resolution to put you first.

'We are your people.'
You write your law of love on our hearts
and we know we belong to you.
You sent your Son, Jesus Christ
to call us to you
and make us one with you.
As your people of love
we long to serve you in the world,
praying and caring for those
who cry out to you in need.
We pray for: the poor and powerless;
                those caught up in war or disaster;
                for ...
and for those who are ill or sorrowful, for ....

Our God, with the help of your Holy Spirit
may we, your people,
live together in love and joy and peace,
to the glory of your name
as we pray and work for your kingdom.

JANUARY – Epiphany

Reading: Matthew 2.1-12

Provide a small dish of pound coins, an oil burner and a candle.

Place the coins on a table.

God of majesty, the wise men presented
the gold of kings to your baby Son,
when they offered him homage.
In our prayers we offer you
the gold of our world:
    the gold that can feed the hungry
    and bring freedom to the powerless;
    the gold we can be reluctant to share
    and may even fight for and steal.
Saving God, accept our gold,
that we may use it
guided by your love.

Place the oil burner on the table and light it.

God of wonder, the wise men presented
the incense of worship to your baby Son,
when they offered him homage.
In our prayers we offer you
the sweet scent of our worship,
together with our life as your Church.
May your Holy Spirit inspire us,
binding us together in love
and giving us an active concern for all humankind.
Saving God, accept the prayers of your people
and help us to fill your world
with the fragrance of your love.

Place the candle on the table and light it.

God with us, the wise men presented
the myrrh of suffering to your baby Son,
when they offered him homage.
In our prayers we bring to you
the suffering of your world:
>the victims of war and hatred ...;
>those struck down by disease or disaster ...;
>those struggling in poverty and hunger ....

We offer you our concern for those who are ill or frail
or sorrowful, for ....
Saving God, you know our pain.
We ask for the hope, peace and comfort
that your love for us can bring.

JANUARY – Octave of Prayer for Christian Unity *(Week 3/4)*

Reading: John 17.6-10, 20-23

Fatherly God, we praise and thank you
for the gift of Jesus Christ our brother;
for his life of teaching and healing
and for his death and rising again
that we might see your likeness in him
and trust you with our lives.

We all belong to you, loving Parent,
but too often we forget.
When we look at other Christians,
whose beliefs or worship differ from ours,
we see only what is different
and not the family resemblance.
Forgive us and open us up to your Spirit
that, becoming one in you, we may be
the answer to Christ's prayer.

We pray for the leaders of our churches
as they talk and pray and work together,
discovering new ways of being one.
We pray for the churches here in
neighbourhood/area/town
as they come together this week to worship you.
Show us how we can best serve this present age
as the united people of God.

We pray for the Church throughout the world,
divided by geography, custom and history,
challenged by different needs and opportunities;
but united by our desire to worship you,
to work and pray for your kingdom.
We remember the Church in ... *(area of concern)*
and pray that ....

Show us how we can best serve this present age
as the united people of God.

Make us one that the world may say
'See how these Christians love one another!'
Make us one that the world may see
its hope of salvation in Jesus Christ.

JANUARY – Vocations *(Week 4)*
Reading: Mark 1.16-20

If appropriate, ask people to spend a few moments in silence considering how God's call to them as Christians affects their daily life and work, and whether God is calling them to new spheres of service.

Loving God, the first disciples
heard the voice of Jesus loud and clear,
calling them to leave their nets
and give their lives to him,
asking them to make
the leap of faith and commitment.

We have heard his call, too,
but not always clearly or with understanding.
Life can offer us many choices
and leave us uncertain and confused
about what we should do,
    why we should do it,
    or what our priorities should be.
We ask for the guidance of your Spirit
to help us respond with faith and wisdom.

We pray for those who are
listening out for Christ's call to them
and for those who have responded to his call
to serve you in a particular way in the world.

We pray for:
    church workers;
    for those working in the medical professions;
    for teachers and those working for social
    services,
    here and in other countries.

We pray for all people of faith who believe
that what they do in their daily work or life
is their response to God's call to them.

Calling God, you have something
for each one of us to do:
open our ears to your call;
open our eyes to the needs around us;
open our hearts to your way of love;
that we may be Christ's true disciples.

JANUARY – World Leprosy Day
Reading: Matthew 8.1-4

During the response people could be encouraged to reach out and touch the arm or shoulder of the person sitting near them, or even hold hands.

All-embracing God, we praise you
because you reach out to us in Christ, touching us
with your love.
We praise you because you long to touch all the
people of your world
with compassion, healing and joy.

L: Loving God, help us to reach out and touch one
    another:
R: **Help us to share your love.**

We pray for those in our world
whom no one wants to reach out and touch:
    we think of those suffering from leprosy;
    of the victims of the AIDS virus;
    and of those struck down by infectious or
        contagious diseases
        that strike fear in their families and friends.
We pray for those who work with and for them
to enable the healing of bodies, minds and spirits,
to offer them hope. We pray for....

L: Loving God, help us to reach out and touch one
    another:
R: **Help us to share your love.**

We pray for those in our society
whom no one wants to reach out and touch:
    we think of the homeless sleeping rough;
    of those disfigured by disease or accident;
    and of those who appear strange or threatening.

We pray for those
who come alongside them in their distress,
seeing through their outer appearance
to the person within,
offering them friendship and understanding,
offering them hope. We pray for ....

L: Loving God, help us to reach out and touch one
    another:
R: Help us to share your love.

We pray for the people we come across
who are in need of warmth and reassurance,
        of acceptance, approval and affection;
        who need to know that they belong.
We think of those who are ill and frightened
        and of those suffering deep hurt because they
        have lost a loved one,
or have been painfully scarred
        by abuse or indifference.
May we offer them friendship, understanding and
        hope.

L: Loving God, help us to reach out and touch one
    another:
R: Help us to share your love.

JANUARY – Holocaust Memorial Day (27 January)

Reading: Psalm 77

Suffering God, at times we find it hard to praise you.
There are things that happen in our world
that we do not even want to think about,
that we would rather pass by on the other side
than make ourselves see and acknowledge.
These are the things we feel are too dreadful to talk
or even pray about, because words are not enough.
In your presence, help us to be brave enough
to remember, in silence, the Holocaust,
its victims and its perpetrators.

Silence

L: In your love and mercy:
R: Hear our prayer.

Transforming God,
we know that you can make all things new
and so we dare to ask for your forgiveness
for the terrible things human beings do to one
another:
> the Holocaust ...;
> other genocides ...;
> the cruelty of the conflicts in ....

When we gaze at your Son, nailed upon the cross,
we know that you share our pain
and that you alone can redeem it.

L: In your love and mercy:
R: Hear our prayer.

We pray for the victims of atrocities
who will always bear the scars of suffering
as they carry the consequences of human sin.
We know that they can never forget
    the evil done to them
but we pray that they may come to forgive the
    evildoer
and not be further burdened
    by bitterness and hatred.

L: In your love and mercy:
R: Hear our prayer.

We pray for the perpetrators and for ourselves
that, with our eyes and imaginations opened up by
    your Spirit,
we may acknowledge our common humanity
with all the peoples of your world.
May the tears of the victims of genocide,
of persecution, warfare and injustice,
be wiped dry by your holy hand forever,
so that we may be a people worthy to praise you.

L: In your love and mercy:
R: Hear our prayer.

FEBRUARY – **Presentation of Christ in the Temple (Candlemas)**

Reading: Luke 2.22-40

God of our lives,
when we look at the state of the world,
of society, community and church,
we can feel weary and disillusioned.
Very little seems to change for the better.
Hope is kindled but quickly fizzles out
like a candle flame lit in a draughty room.
New ideas are born, but 'we've seen it all before'
and we feel old and sad and needy.
In the cold dark days of February we ask
'Where is the hopeful joy of Christmas?'

In our weariness we pray:
help us to be like the aged Simeon and Anna,
who watched and prayed, ready to receive
the new gift that you had for Israel.
Open our eyes to see again the Christ-child
come to the Temple of your people.
Fill us with thanksgiving.

We pray for the peoples of the world,
who watch and pray for signs of hope:
for an end to war and conflict;
for justice and freedom;
for a fair return for their labour;
for a better future for their children.
We pray for ....

We pray for the peoples of your Church
who watch and pray for signs of hope:
for spiritual renewal and growth;
for a clear vision to guide them;
for a spirit of unity, respect and understanding;
for new ways of reaching hearts and minds.

We pray for those we know wearied by illness or
sorrow, for ....

Help us to be open to your coming to us
in new and unfamiliar ways.
Keep us faithful to you through the difficult days,
ready to embrace new opportunities
to share your love,
in the name of Jesus Christ, the hope of the world.

FEBRUARY – National Marriage Week
(Week 7)
Reading: Matthew 19.4-6

We praise you, creative God,
for making us male and female in your image;
for giving us one another
to be companions, lovers and friends.

L: God, come into our relationships:
R: And bless them with your love.

We praise you, saving God,
for coming in your Son to live among us
to share the experience of human living
and be loved and nourished in an earthly home.

L: God, come into our relationships:
R: And bless them with your love.

We praise you, sustaining God,
for filling our hearts with love for one another
and inspiring the kindness, self-control and
        faithfulness
that we need in our closest relationships.

L: God, come into our relationships:
R: And bless them with your love.

We are sorry that we often find it so hard
to make the good relationships you ask of us.
We are sorry that we are self-centred and
        self-righteous
and sometimes foolish and unfeeling.

L: God, come into our relationships:
R: And bless them with your love.

We pray for those just starting out
on the new adventure of married life:
that they might find joy and fulfilment together
and learn to look after and encourage one another.

L: God, come into our relationships:
R: And bless them with your love.

We pray for those in troubled marriages.
May they feel your healing touch on their wounds,
on feelings of betrayal, rejection and loss.
Give them hope for a new and better future.

L: God, come into our relationships:
R: And bless them with your love.

We pray for the children of broken marriages,
often bewildered, hurt and insecure.
Give their parents the wisdom and love they need
to help their children through the difficult times.

L: God, come into our relationships:
R: And bless them with your love.

You have made us for one another, and we thank you.

L: God, come into our relationships:
R: And bless them with your love.

FEBRUARY – Education *(Week 7)*
Reading: Matthew 7.24-29

God of wonder and wisdom,
we praise and thank you
for the myriad truths you reveal to us.

We learn from your world:
> which reveals to us your provision for your
> > creatures
> and your love of beauty, order and design;
> which reveals to us our own responsibility
> to care for all you have entrusted to us.

We learn from your Son, Jesus Christ:
> who reveals to us your love for humankind
> and your offer of life in all its fullness;
> who reveals to us our own responsibility
> to respond with repentance, faith and
> > discipleship.

We learn from your Holy Spirit:
> who reveals to us your presence in the world
> and the transforming power of your love;
> who reveals to us our own responsibility
> to be open to your guidance, promptings and
> > inspiration.

We are sorry, Teacher God, for not listening properly.
Help us to pay attention to you
and to build our lives on the rock of your teaching.

We pray for those engaged in learning,
that they may make the most of their opportunities
and find joy and excitement in their studies.
We pray for those who teach,
that they may share their knowledge
with insight, enthusiasm and commitment.

We pray for those struggling in education:
pupils finding it hard to keep up;
teachers faced with unruly and uninterested classes;
schools under pressure to achieve,
but under-resourced and under-supported.

We have so much to learn, loving God,
about the world, one another, and you.
May we be eager to find you in everything
and our lives be enlightened
      by your glorious presence.

FEBRUARY – Week of Friendship *(Week 8)*
Reading: Mark 2.1-5

Loving God,
we thank you for the gift of friendship:
    for the friends in Christ here with us today;
    for the friends where we live or work;
    for old friends, near or far away.
Most of all, we praise and thank you
    for the friendship of your Son, Jesus Christ,
    our ever-present companion and Saviour
    who fills our lives with love, joy and peace.

L: For the gift of friendship:
R: We thank you.

We thank you for the sharing within friendship:
    the confiding and supporting and discussing.
In silence we recall
happy times and occasions shared with our friends ....

Silence

We also recall the sad and painful experiences we
    have shared ....

Silence

L: For the gift of friendship:
R: We thank you.

We thank you for the caring within friendship:
    the affection, understanding and willing help.
In silence we recall
the ways in which our friends have cared for us ....

Silence

We also bring to mind
the faces and names of friends
needing our care today.

Silence

L: For the gift of friendship:
R: We thank you.

Healing God,
we think how the friends of the paralysed man carried
  him to Jesus;
and how Jesus used their love and faith
  to make him whole.
In faith, we bring to you
our friends who are ill, frail, sorrowful or anxious.
We pray for ...
asking for your healing and strengthening touch
  upon their lives.

L: For the gift of friendship:
R: We thank you.

FEBRUARY – St Valentine's Day (14 February)

Reading: Song of Solomon 2.8-13

Have a display of roses, cards etc. and play suitable music.

God, whose name is Love, we rejoice today
as we celebrate your gift of romantic love:
a love that causes hearts to leap
    songs to be sung;
    self to be forgotten;
a love that brings new colour into human lives.

We praise you for the joys of romantic love:
    the joy of delight in one another;
    the joy of belonging;
    the joy of shared pleasure.

We praise you for the creativity of romantic love:
    the music, art and poetry;
    the building up of one another;
    the birth of family life.

We praise you for the generosity of romantic love:
    the sharing of affection and care;
    the supplying of deep needs;
    the desire to give oneself.

Our God, you love humankind
with the passion and devotion of a lover.
In Christ you risked yourself
to bring us back to you.
We pray for those who have risked loving
and have been hurt:
    whose love has not been returned;
    who are caught up in destructive relationships;
    who have been betrayed.

We pray, too, for those who have sought love
 but have never found it.
You, Source of Love, know our needs and desires;
help us to open our hearts and lives to you
and your perfect love.

FEBRUARY/MARCH – Shrove Tuesday
Reading: Luke 9.51-62

> The breaking of eggs,
> the beating of batter,
> the sizzling of melting butter,
> the tossing of pancakes:
> another Shrove Tuesday.

Ever-present God,
we thank you for the joyful rituals
with which we embroider our lives;
but we confess
that we often forget why we do what we do
and do not make the effort to remember.
We do not prepare ourselves properly
for the special days of our faith.

This Shrove Tuesday we ask
for the help of your Holy Spirit
that we may be prepared
for the coming weeks of Lent.

Help us to really concentrate,
to focus our minds and hearts and lives on you.
Help us to push behind us those things
that distract us from following Christ to Jerusalem.

We want to remember it all.
We want to take part, to be there too.
We want Lent to be a time of blessing
for us and all your people.

When the pancakes are all eaten
and the pans washcd and put away,
we will start on the journey to Jerusalem,
sustained by our faith and prayers.
May we know you travelling with us
along Christ's way of suffering love.

FEBRUARY/MARCH – Ash Wednesday
Reading: Matthew 6.1-6

Ask those present to write down on pieces of paper what they are giving up or taking up for Lent. These will be placed in a bowl during the prayer.

All-seeing God,
you know us through and through.
We cannot hide ourselves from you.

L: God of Love, we confess all that we are to you:
R: Forgive us and save us.

We try to hide our faults and flaws
from others, ourselves and you.
We try to hide away the parts of us
we believe are unacceptable to you.
We cover ourselves up with our religion.

L: God of Love, we confess all that we are to you:
R: Forgive us and save us.

We try to shut out
the painful demands of your love
that probe into our innermost souls.
We try to shut out
your voice with the noise of our own busyness.
We try to ignore you.

L: God of Love, we confess all that we are to you:
R: Forgive us and save us.

This Lent, make us aware
of your loving presence in our lives
through the daily reminders
of the things we have given up or taken up.
We offer them to you in prayer ....

The pledges are put in the bowl followed by a period of silence.

This Lent, embracing God,
we offer our whole selves to you:
the things we like and the things which shame us.
Repenting of our failings,
we acknowledge our need of you
and so rejoice in the saving love we see in Jesus.

L: God of Love, we confess all that we are to you:
R: Forgive us and save us.

FEBRUARY/MARCH – Lent 1

Reading: 1 John 1.8 – 2.2

God of forgiveness, we worship and adore you.
We long for our lives to show
that we are your faithful and obedient people.

L: In your love and mercy:
R: Hear our prayer.

But when we turn from looking
at your love and mercy for us
to looking at our own lives,
we see how far short we fall
from obeying your commands to love.
Sick at heart, we come to you
to ask for your forgiveness.

L: In your love and mercy:
R: Hear our prayer.

We have sinned as members of the human race,
in our care for your world.
We confess the violence and greed,
the injustice, selfishness and exploitation,
that spoil your creation.
We pray for ....
We ask forgiveness for the sins of the human race.

L: In your love and mercy:
R: Hear our prayer.

We have sinned as members of your Church
in our weak witness to your love.
We confess our divisions and disagreements,
our apathy and fear of change.
We pray for ....

We ask forgiveness for the sins of the Church.

L: In your love and mercy:
R: Hear our prayer.

We have sinned as your children
by not being the people you want us to be.
We confess our selfishness towards others,
our unfeeling behaviour and shallow thinking.
We bring our own personal shortcomings to you ....

Silence

We ask forgiveness for our daily sins.

L: In your love and mercy:
R: Hear our prayer.

FEBRUARY/MARCH – Lent 2   27 · 3 11
Reading: Luke 18.10-14

Creator God, we praise you,
because you love us, delight in us and care for us,
despite our shortcomings.
Saviour God, we praise you,
because you love us to the uttermost,
offering us forgiveness and new life in you.
Spirit of God, we praise you,
because you pour your love into our hearts,
assuring, encouraging and remaking us.

We praise you, but sadly we admit that
our praise often comes from heavy hearts
burdened by a sense of our own sinfulness.

We confess that we want to be in control
of our lives and our salvation,
and are oppressed by a sense of hopelessness
when our endeavours to be good fail.
Help us to acknowledge
that our deepest need is our need for you.
Give us the true humility
that looks to you in confidence
for loving forgiveness and help.

May this Lent be a time
of inner peace and joyful prayer,
and the casting off of burdens
of guilt and hopelessness;
so that we may then be ready to accept
the gracious gifts of Passiontide and Easter.

Then we will see,
    with heads no longer bowed down by despair,
our sin and suffering carried
    on the cross for us by Christ,
and the glorious victory of Easter Day.

MARCH – World Day of Prayer *(First Friday)*
Reading: Psalm 66.1-9

This prayer could be used at preparation meetings before the World Day of Prayer or at a meeting after the event, with the appropriate change of tenses.

God, our God,
in our many different languages,
as people of different races and cultures,
we gather to worship you together, *(today)*.
Young and old, poor and rich, women and men,
we gather to worship you together, *(today)*.
On every continent, in every time zone,
we gather to worship you together, *(today)*.

L: Let all the earth praise our God:
R: Amen, amen.

God of the nations, we thank you for the
opportunities of this day:

>   for discovering afresh that we belong to your
>   worldwide family
>   made one in Christ our Saviour;

>   for the joy of offering worship prepared
>   by Christian women from ... *(name of country)*;

>   for the privilege of receiving their insights
>   and sharing in their joys and pains.

We pray for them and the church in ... *(name of country)*

>   for ... *(special needs of the people)*.

L: Let all the earth praise our God:
R: Amen, amen.

All-seeing God, we thank you for opening our eyes
to a larger vision
of what our faith means to the world.
Help us to treasure this vision
and to be more deeply aware of one another's needs
so that we may work together for the coming on earth
of your kingdom of justice and peace, love and joy.

L: Let all the earth praise our God:
R: Amen, amen.

MARCH – World Environment Week
(Week 10)
Reading: Psalm 8.3-9

Ask people to think about how they have experienced the beauty of creation recently, and to share those sights and sounds. Then ask them what they have seen or heard that has spoilt creation's beauty. During the prayer there will be times of silence to enable them to reflect on their experiences.

Generous God,
when we look at the world you have given us,
we see beauty, bounty and infinite possibility,
a creation full of wonder and delight.

Silence

You have given us so much that is good,
but we have responded to your gifts
like spoilt children,
loving them only for what we could get out of them:
> we have grabbed greedily at the earth's
> resources;
>> at land and forest;
>> at fish, animals and birds;
> with no thought for the future
>> of our children or the children of the poor.

Silence

Like spoilt children, we have not looked after
the things that you have entrusted to us.
We have polluted the air and water,
> making dust bowls of good earth
> and damaging the precious ozone layer;
> with no thought for the future
>> of our children or the children of the poor.

Silence

We are sorry, loving God.
Please forgive us and guide us
into better ways of living in our environment
before it is too late.

Silence

We pray for those who work and campaign
for a better stewardship of the earth's resources.
Help us to support them by doing what we can.
As we wait in hope for the redemption of all creation,
through the saving love of your Son, Jesus Christ,
grant us the maturity to treat your world
with the respect it deserves.

MARCH – Fairtrade Fortnight *(Weeks 10 &11)*
Reading: Isaiah 58.3c-7

If possible, arrange to have a small Fairtrade stall.

Each of us, loving God,
wants justice for ourselves.
We expect to be treated fairly,
    yet with allowances made for our weaknesses.
We want fairness in our family relationships,
    in our communities;
    in our country;
    in our world.
Help us, in our search for justice,
to look beyond our own needs to the needs of others.

L: This is our prayer:
R: **Help us to know and to do your will.**

Each of us, listening God,
demands to be paid fairly for the work we do,
    enough to pay for the essentials for life;
but the poor of your world who work long and hard,
    and yet still do not earn enough to feed their
        children,
have voices too weak to make demands.
Help us, in our search for justice,
to hear not only our own voices,
but the voices of the powerless.

L: This is our prayer:
R: **Help us to know and to do your will.**

We thank you, God of justice,
for the work of the Fairtrade organisations, for ...
who offer justice and new opportunities
    to the exploited and poor producers of our world.
We thank you that they offer ways in which we, too,
can take part in the struggle for justice and life
to which you call your people.

We pray for ... *(any special local or church projects and those involved).*

Help us to support Fairtrade
with our prayers and concerned interest
and with our campaigning and buying power,
as we work for your kingdom
of justice, hope and love.

L: This is our prayer:
R: Help us to know and to do your will.

MARCH – Refugee Week *(Week 11)*
Reading: Matthew 25.31-46

Display suitable pictures and newspaper clippings. There will be a time of silence during this prayer, as we imagine what it is like to be a refugee.

Shelter, food and drink,
safety, community and care:
these are things we need, our God,
to live as your children in your world.

But in so many countries
people are denied the basics for human life:
they are victims of greed and injustice
of warfare and persecution;
we watch streams of frightened people
forced to leave behind all that they have known
and most of what they own
because they fear for their own lives
and the lives of their children.
You know, God, how these sights distress us,
how we long to close our eyes to them
and our ears to their cries for help.
We are saddened, but do not want our lives disturbed
by their demands.

Forgive us, loving God, and remind us again
of the teaching of our Saviour, Jesus Christ,
that the common humanity we share with him
is also our common humanity with those in need.

Help us, as we pray for refugees,
to reflect on how we also would suffer
if forced to leave our homes and land.

Silence

May the common humanity that we share
bring understanding to our prayers
and generosity of spirit to our giving.

We pray for the refugees from ...
for those who seek asylum
	and a new life in this country;
for the work of UNHCR,
	the United Nations refugee agency.

Silence

Christ who was homeless, bless the wanderers.
Christ who was hungry, bless the needy.
Christ who was crucified, bless the fearful.
Christ who was raised to life on Easter Day,
grant freedom and hope to suffering humankind.

MARCH – Comic Relief Day (Third Friday)
Reading: Ecclesiastes 3.1-8

Comforting God,
you have consoled us with the promise
that, at the end, you will wipe away all tears.

L: God who smiles upon us,
      turn our tears of suffering
R: Into the laughter of joy.

We pray for the work of Comic Relief:
      in wiping away tears of despair
            with the offer of hope and help;
      in deepening our understanding of need
      and offering us the joyful opportunity to give.

L: God who smiles upon us,
      turn our tears of suffering
R: Into the laughter of joy.

This is the time, God of our lives,
'to weep and to laugh',
to look into the eyes of one of your children
      and see the longing to be free to enjoy life
            and the longing to share in laughter.

L: God who smiles upon us,
      turn our tears of suffering
R: Into the laughter of joy.

God of power, like a fool, you risked everything
when, in Christ, you shared our humanity
and made yourself vulnerable to rejection and pain.
But it was by the foolishness of the cross
      that we have been saved.

L: God who smiles upon us,
      turn our tears of suffering
R: Into the laughter of joy.

Help us to be fools for you, loving God.
Help us to love, live and give
with the generosity of fools,
that there may be laughter in heaven
and glory to you on earth.

MARCH – Mothering Sunday
Reading: Psalm 139.13-18

Loving God, we worship you
for loving us like a mother loves her children:
    as Creator, you care for our needs,
        giving us the world to be our home,
        providing us with food, shelter and a family;
    as Saviour, you make our lives good,
        healing us and teaching us,
        helping us to grow to spiritual maturity;
    as Spirit you bring harmony to our lives
        filling us with inner security and peace,
        enabling us to live as your true children.

L: In your love and mercy:
R: Hear our prayer.

We thank you for the nurturing love
we have received from others:
    from our mothers, family members and friends;
    from Mother Church;
and we pray for all those who mother us ....

Silence

L: In your love and mercy:
R: Hear our prayer.

We thank you that we can offer
a motherly care like yours to others:
    loving them unconditionally;
    meeting their physical and emotional needs;
and we pray for those we mother, especially within
our families ....

Silence

L: In your love and mercy:
R: Hear our prayer.

We pray for those who have not received
the motherly love that they need:
>   those whose mothers have died or left home;
>   those who have been neglected or abused;
>   those with mothers physically or mentally ill ....

Silence

L: In your love and mercy:
R: Hear our prayer.

We pray for those caring for their own mothers
because they are sick, old or infirm ....

Silence

L: In your love and mercy:
R: Hear our prayer.

We pray for mothers torn apart by the sufferings of
their children:
>   through war ...
>   through poverty ...
>   through illness ....

Silence

L: In your love and mercy:
R: Hear our prayer.

Loving God, we thank you that in Jesus
you have come close to us like a mother.

MARCH/APRIL – Palm Sunday into Holy Week
Reading: Mark 11.1-10

Distribute palm crosses to be held during the prayer.

God of joyful hope,
we celebrate your royal promises
as we recollect Christ's triumphal, palm-strewn entry
into Jerusalem.

Silence

God of strange and amazing truth,
we see your majesty in that joyous interlude
before the real and awe-full business of Holy Week.

This paradox of a cross made from a palm leaf
makes us wonder if we know what is happening
         any more than did the crowds in Jerusalem
         or the executioners at Golgotha.

Silence

God of forgiveness, we confess
that sometimes our acts of worship
are more about making ourselves feel good
than meeting the all-consuming reality of your love.

Silence

This Holy Week, help us to focus
on the Good News of salvation in Christ;
we ask you to fill our hearts and minds
         with its meaning.
We want to keep faith with Jesus,
         to walk with him along the painful path of true
         love.
We want to acknowledge our part in the sin
         that put him on the cross.

We want to feel the pulsating joy
of your resurrection victory over evil and death.

Silence

As we hold our palm crosses
we offer you our praise:
you paid the price
and prepared the way for us
through your eternal love.

MARCH/APRIL – Maundy Thursday
Reading: John 13.1-17

Creator God, we thank and praise you
because you do not hold back from loving us;
you took the risk of conceiving humankind
and, in your generosity, gave us all that we need,
asking of us only that we love you and one another.

L: Lord, who kneels and washes our feet:
R: Teach us to love and serve.

Saviour God, we thank and praise you
because you do not hold back from loving us;
you took the risk of sharing our human life
and, in your generosity, gave that life for us,
asking of us only that we love you and one another.

L: Lord, who kneels and washes our feet:
R: Teach us to love and serve.

Spirit of God, we thank and praise you
because you do not hold back from loving us;
you take the risk of going unnoticed
as you live and move in our lives and world
asking of us only that we open ourselves
to your power.

L: Lord, who kneels and washes our feet:
R: Teach us to love and serve.

Loving God, we confess to you
that we do not live our lives
in full response to your love.
Our feet are dirty and need to be washed by you.
Everywhere there are
people with feet soiled and wearied
by their walk through life:

those whose physical or spiritual needs drag
them down;
those with lives sullied by illness, anxiety or
sorrow.
We pray for ....
Help us not to hold back from showing love
to those who need it the most.

L: Lord, who kneels and washes our feet:
R: Teach us to love and serve.

MARCH/APRIL – Good Friday

Reading: Mark 15.20b-39 (or Mark 15.6-39)

Place a cross somewhere prominent and ask those present to reflect on it and on the feelings of the first disciples on Good Friday.

Silence

Nothing can prepare us, loving God,
for the reality of this day.
We, Christ's disciples,
had not wanted to understand
that the Day of our Lord
would be like this.

Nothing can prepare us
for the reality of evil.
We do not want to know
that those healing hands were nailed to the cross;
 or that children can be taken away and killed;
 or that whole ethnic groups can be exterminated.

Nothing can prepare us
for the reality of suffering.
We do not want to hear
Christ's cry of desolation from the cross;
 or the moaning of sick people in pain;
 or the sobbing of the mothers of hungry children.

Nothing can prepare us, loving God,
for the reality of death.
We do not want to witness
Christ's parting from us;
 or the last breath of someone we love;
 or our own mortality.

Nothing can prepare us
for the realities of Good Friday,
and only you, loving God, can console us
with the fulfilment of our hopes on Easter Day.

MARCH/APRIL – Easter
Reading: Mark 16.1-8

God of surprises,
we worship you now
as we celebrate the biggest surprise of all.

L: The Lord is risen:
R: He is risen indeed! Alleluia!

Like his disciples,
we have walked with Jesus
through the gospel stories.
We have listened to his teaching;
we have seen him heal those in need
and we have come to know him in our hearts.
And then we saw him taken away,
cruelly treated and killed.
Black night fell on our souls
until the sun rose on Easter Day.

L: The Lord is risen:
R: He is risen indeed! Alleluia!

God of hope,
our faith in you is restored:
we know that not even evil and death
can separate us from your love.

L: The Lord is risen:
R: He is risen indeed! Alleluia!

God of joy,
there is laughter on our lips
and deep peace in our hearts
as we greet our belovèd risen Jesus.

L: The Lord is risen:
R: He is risen indeed! Alleluia!

God of love,
in Jesus you have done for us
more than we could expect or can understand.
In thanks, we offer ourselves to you.

L: The Lord is risen:
R: He is risen indeed! Alleluia!

God of our salvation,
with the help of your Holy Spirit
we will share with the world, by word and deed,
the Good News of our risen Saviour.

L: The Lord is risen:
R: He is risen indeed! Alleluia!

APRIL – World Health Day (7 April)

Reading: Mark 1.29-34a

Ask those present to be silent, to become aware of their own bodies: breathing, pulse and senses as well as aches, pains and rumblings!

Creator God, we praise you,
for we are wonderfully made.
We thank you for the ways in which
the different parts of our bodies
work together to keep us alive;
to fill our lives with opportunities
to be and experience and do.
Help us to cherish our health and strength
by offering ourselves to you.

We also want to offer ourselves to you
at times when we are neither well nor strong,
asking that you will use these times
to draw us closer to you.
May our feelings of weakness
make us more sensitive
to the suffering and frustration
of the victims of sickness and injury.

God of healing and wholeness,
just as the sick drew close to Jesus
and his healing, comforting touch,
we draw near to you in prayer,
praying about our own illnesses and infirmities
and others for whom we feel concern.
We pray for ....
We think of the millions all over the world
made ill by poverty, ignorance and war;
those unable to receive the treatment they need
to save and transform their lives
and the lives of their children.

Help us to remember them
in our prayers and our giving
and to challenge those with power and influence
to develop policies that can help them.
God of healing and wholeness,
who desires only good things for your children,
we pray for health for your world.

APRIL – Mental Health Action Week
(Week 17)

Reading: 1 Samuel 18.10-16

God of healing and wholeness,
we know that you desire good health for humankind
and so we pray in faith
for all those struggling with mental ill-health:
for those whose lives are blighted
by their different perceptions of reality
and their disturbing behaviour.

Living among us, in our community, we see
people of all ages battling with mental illness:
 the tiny child with attention deficit disorder;
 the teenager in the grips of anorexia;
 the young man with schizophrenia;
 the young mother with post-natal depression;
 the middle-aged man
  having a nervous breakdown;
 the grandmother with Alzheimer's disease.

We pray for ....

Loving God, we would like a world where those with
mental illness
are treated with understanding and respect;
where they, and those who care for them,
are given all the help and support they need.
We would like to see further advances being made
in scientific knowledge and in treatment.

This is what we pray for,
but we also confess to you
that we and our society are sick
with the ignorance and fear
that stigmatise those with mental illness,
undervaluing and rejecting them.

Give us the transforming help of your Holy Spirit,
that we may see the God-given value
    of every human life
and offer health-giving love to our needy world.
Help us to accept one another;
    to soothe the distressed;
    to encourage the downhearted;
    and to seek fulfilment for everyone.

MAY – The Ascension of Christ

Reading: Acts 1.1-11

During this prayer, those present will be asked to hold hands.

God of today, yesterday and tomorrow,
we find it very hard to let go of much in our lives;
we want to hold on to what we love
like the disciples who held on to the ascending Jesus
with their heaven-cast eyes.

But, let go from human constraints,
Christ became alive to his people for evermore,
and the power of your Holy Spirit was released
to move through the world, making things new.

Loving God, we ask that you help us to learn to let go
of all that stops us giving ourselves to you,
that stops your Spirit working through us.
Help us to let go of the old ways
that hold us back from following you
into a challenging future.
Help us to let go
        as individuals;
        as your people, the Church;
        as human beings living in a complex world.
Help us, for we find it so very hard.

We remember how some of Christ's disciples
desperately sought his reassuring touch
when they met their risen Lord.
We, too, seek his touch on our lives
and thank you that we can experience it
in the loving touch we give one another.
Let us, in Christ, hold hands together ... *(hold hands)*

We feel safe and peaceful together in your presence,
but, loving God, you challenge us to let go.
You challenge us to leave behind the safety
we find here
and go out with you into your world
to release the touch of Christ into other needy lives.
We loose hands to free them to serve you.
(release hands)
Help us, God of today, yesterday and tomorrow,
for we do not want to hold you back.

MAY – Christian Aid Week *(Week 20)*
Reading: Psalm 146.5-9

Our God, we praise and thank you
for the abundant love you pour out upon us:
    for giving us this world to provide for our needs;
    for giving us free will so that we can choose
      to express our humanity
      by loving you and one another;
    and for giving us yourself in Christ,
    who became one with us
    that we might become one with you.

L: Loving God, we pray:
R: Help us to know and to do your will.

In sorrow we confess to you
the ways in which we have misused your gifts to us.
We confess:
    our greedy use of the world's resources;
    the ways in which we have exercised our freedom
      to turn away from you
      and your commandments to love;
    our failure to make the good news of Jesus
    good news for the lives of everyone.

L: Loving God, we pray:
R: Help us to know and to do your will.

Help us, by the power of your Holy Spirit,
to turn away from our foolishness and selfishness
and commit ourselves again to establishing
your kingdom on earth,
the kingdom of God
    where men, women and children
      are truly valued;
    where injustice, oppression and hatred
      are but distant memories;

where poverty, hunger, ignorance and disease
   do not stop children from growing
   to their full stature.

L: Loving God, we pray:
R: Help us to know and to do your will.

We pray for the work of Christian Aid
with suffering and needy people
throughout the world
regardless of their religion or race.
We pray for the work in ... (or the situation in ...).
We thank you that Christian Aid has offered
life before death to so many,
and given hope to those who knew only despair.
We pledge ourselves, in the name of Jesus,
who came to offer life in all its fullness,
to support all those who work for Christian Aid
with our prayers and by our giving.

L: Loving God, we pray:
R: Help us to know and to do your will.

MAY – International Day of the Family (15 May)

Reading: Ephesians 3.14-19

God, our heavenly Father and Mother,
we thank you for families:
> for the family of humankind rich in its diversity;
> for the family of the Church,
>   sisters and brothers in Jesus;
> for our own families and the love that we share.

Family life can be heaven, loving God,
but at times it can be hell.
We bring to you in prayer
family relationships in trouble:
we pray for our world family where
> country hates country,
> race hates race,
> religion hates religion,
and there is no sense of belonging to one another.
We pray for the Church family
where different beliefs and traditions
set Christ's sisters and brothers against one another
as they try to prove they love you best;
we pray for families we know
where there is argument, anger or abuse,
asking that family love might survive.

Silence

We thank you, loving God, for those families
where young and old are built up by love
and shown affection, respect and understanding.
We pray that such family life be valued and upheld.

We share with you the pain we feel
when we see a family in difficulty;
cracking under the strain and stress
of broken relationships, illness, poverty
or worry about the behaviour of a family member.
We pray for those hurt or damaged by family life:
    those unloved, unwanted or abused;
    those deformed by unwise or selfish loving.

God, our heavenly Father and Mother,
we pray that human family life may be shaped
by the power that you reveal to us
in your Son, Jesus Christ.

MAY – Amnesty International Day (28 May)

Reading: Isaiah 61.1-3

If possible, have an Amnesty candle on display, or suitable pictures/posters.

God of justice, giver of courage,
we praise you for the strength you give us
in the face of evil.
We praise you that, just like a candle flame
that continues to shine through the bars of a prison,
the human spirit that you have given us
is not extinguished by hatred or suffering.

L: For those held captive by injustice and fear:
R: We pray for freedom and peace.

We pray for those held in prison today
because of their political or religious beliefs;
we pray for ....
We pray for all those who risk torture
by speaking out against injustice and tyranny.
We pray for those who,
with their friends and families,
face persecution, harassment and even death
because they refuse to compromise with evil.

L: For those held captive by injustice and fear:
R: We pray for freedom and peace.

We thank you, loving God,
for the work of Amnesty International
in forcing ordinary people and those in power
to face up to the reality of such suffering,
and to respond to the challenge of that reality.

L: For those held captive by injustice and fear:
R: We pray for freedom and peace.

You are a God of justice, freedom and love.
Yours are the values we want for our world.
Help us to pursue those values and live by them.
Help us to support those willing to die for them.

MAY/JUNE – Pentecost

Reading: Acts 2.1-4

Holy Spirit,
you came like a roaring wind,
unseen, powerful and noisy.
Your coming must have shaken the safe house
where Christ's disciples prayed and hid.
Blow into your safe Church, we pray,
and make a noise to wake and shake us.
Disturb our sheltered quiet
and fill us with your exciting energy.

Silence

Holy Spirit,
you came like bright flames of fire
to settle on Christ's fear-chilled disciples.
Your coming must have lit up the safe house
where they sat in the darkness of indecision.
Set our hearts alight, we pray,
and fire us up with the power of God's love,
so that we may warm
the heart of our cold world.

Silence

Holy Spirit,
you came as an interpreter,
loosening the tongues of Christ's people.
Your coming must have filled the safe house
with the strange and lovely language of praise.
Inspire our tongues, we pray.
Give us the words that we need
to speak hope and comfort to those who suffer.
Give us the language we need
to speak of the good news of new life in Christ
to those with ears deafened by materialism
and the cynical clamour of the present age.

Silence

Come, Holy Spirit, and blow new life
into your Church and your world.

MAY/JUNE – Trinity

Reading: Matthew 28.16-20

Creator God,
we praise you for your awe-inspiring majesty
and thank you for the riches and beauty of creation
inspired and brought to being by your love.
We pray for the world, sharing our concerns
for countries where there is:
> war, for ...;
> conflict and unrest, for ...;
> natural disaster, for ...;
> famine, for ...;
> or disease, for ....

Creator God, guide the nations and their leaders
with your love and mercy.

L: Creator, Saviour and Holy Spirit:
R: Hear our prayer.

Saviour God,
we praise you for your deep and indestructible love
and thank you for coming to share
our human life with us
so that we might share
the joys of eternal life with you.
We pray for those needing to feel your touch
upon their lives
because they seek comfort, healing,
forgiveness or strength.
We pray for people we know who are
> ill, for...;
> sorrowful, for ...;
> anxious, for ...;
> and for ....

Saviour God, soothe the lives of those who suffer
with your love and mercy.

L: Creator, Saviour and Holy Spirit:
R: Hear our prayer.

Spirit of God,
we praise you for your amazing, life-changing power
and thank you for the love
that makes and shapes the Church,
filling your people with a joyful need
to worship and serve.
We pray for your church throughout the world,
asking that we might uphold one another
in times of difficulty
and learn from one another's example
and discoveries.
We pray for Church communities:
    anxious about their future;
    challenged by the needs around them;
    seeking to mend broken relationships;
    embarking on new projects.
We pray for ....
Spirit of God, bless the life of your Church with your
love and mercy.

L: Creator, Saviour and Holy Spirit:
R: Hear our prayer.

JUNE – National Carers' Week *(Week 24)*
Reading: Ruth 1.5b-18

Creator God, you designed us for one another,
for companionship, love, nurture and care.
When we read of the life of Jesus,
a life of your love in action,
we see your love for us writ large on every page.
We see you:
> healing those who were sick;
> enabling those with disabilities;
> befriending those who were outcast;
> calming those who were disturbed;
> welcoming the children.

L: Faithful God, we pray for carers:
**R: Uphold them with your strong and patient
love.**

We pray for those whose vocation it is to care,
for those who work in:
> hospitals and hospices;
> residential homes;
> care in the community schemes.

We pray for ... *(names of workers known to the
group)*
and ask that these carers may find joy, satisfaction
and a sense of worth in what they do.
May they be shown appreciation and support
by the people and communities
among whom they work.

L: Faithful God, we pray for carers:
**R: Uphold them with your strong and patient
love.**

We pray for those caring for loved ones at home.
We pray for the parents of children with:
    chronic illnesses;
    terminal diseases;
    demanding disabilities;
    severe behavioural problems.
We pray for children responsible for the care
of their incapacitated parents
and their younger brothers and sisters.
We pray for families caring for their elderly:
    through illness or disability;
    through confusion;
    through their last days.
We pray for ...
asking that their love for one another
might hold them together
through the struggles of their lives.
Make us sensitive to the needs of those who care
and ready to help them however we can.

L: Faithful God, we pray for carers:
R: Uphold them with your strong and patient love.

JUNE – Fathers' Day (Third Sunday)
Reading: Luke 11.1-13 (or Luke 11.11-13)

Loving God, we remember how
Jesus called you Father, or even Dad,
and encouraged his disciples to do the same.
We praise you for being a God
who is as close to us, your children, as a father;
and as constant in your love
as the best of parents can be.

L: Our Father:
R: Hallowed be your name.

We think about our dads
and those who have acted as fathers to us.
We thank you for all they mean to us
and for the good they have contributed to our lives.

Silence

We thank you for them and rejoice in knowing
that your love is even deeper and wiser than theirs.

L: Our Father:
R: Hallowed be your name.

When we look at you, loving God,
we realise how often our human parenting falls short
and how much we need your forgiveness
and your continuing guidance.
We pray for fathers who are struggling with their role
and for children
physically, emotionally or psychologically
        damaged by their fathers,
asking that you might strengthen and heal them.

L: Our Father:
R: Hallowed be your name.

We pray for fathers all over the world
who, however hard they work,
are unable to provide their families
with the safety and shelter they need,
with food, education or medicine.
We pray for those anxious for their children
because they are ill, in trouble or unhappy.
Help us to show care and support
to the struggling fathers of your world.

L: Our Father:
R: Hallowed be your name.

JUNE – National Quiet Week *(Week 25)*
Reading: 1 Kings 19.7-13

God of peace, we long for times of quiet,
to get away from the noise of everyday life;
to leave behind the cacophony of the streets
and the never-ending demands for our attention.
We long for opportunities
to rest in the embrace of blessèd silence.

Silence

Help us, living God,
to respect the times of silence that you give us
and not to try to drown the quiet out
with loud music or broadcast babble.
Help us not to run away from the quiet
because we are afraid to meet ourselves
or to come face to face with your awesome presence.

Silence

Teach us, loving God,
actively to seek quiet times and places
for drawing closer to you
and offering those prayers
that cannot be expressed in words.
Teach us how to be quiet
both on our own and with one another
so that our lives and relationships
may be enriched by your peace.

Silence

We want to take the risk, challenging God,
of meeting you in the silence
and listening to your still, small voice.

Silence

JULY – NCH *(Week 29)*
Reading Matthew 18.2-7

This prayer could be adapted for other children's charities. Have a small display of pictures, information and/or small items associated with childhood.

Living God,
we thank you for the mysterious gift of life.
We do not ask to be born,
yet one day we are aware of our existence
and we know what it is to be happy and comfortable,
what it is to feel need and pain.

Loving God,
because of their vulnerability
we feel anxious for children
and so we bring their needs to you.
You have entrusted them to an adult world
where there is love, wisdom and generosity
but also weakness, ignorance and cruelty;
we need the help and guidance of your Spirit
if our children are to grow up healthy and fulfilled.

Enabling God,
we thank you for the wise and caring work
done by NCH (or charities such as ...)
We pray for the help they give to children at risk:
    family centres;
    treatment for those abused;
    foster care and adoption;
    special schools.

L: In your love and mercy:
R: Hear our prayer.

We pray for the support given to families:
>   community centres;
>   short-break projects;
>   mediation in family break-ups.

L: In your love and mercy:
R: Hear our prayer.

We pray for the provisions made for young people at
risk:
>   leaving-care services;
>   projects for youth justice and homelessness;
>   projects to prevent school exclusions and
>   truancy.

L: In your love and mercy:
R: Hear our prayer.

God, our father and our mother,
we do not ask to be born,
but we ask in prayer that we may all be loved.

JULY – Seafarers *(Week 29)*
Reading: Psalm 107.23-31

Play some sea music or sounds of the sea and ask those present to close their eyes and picture the sea in one of its many moods.

Creator God,
when we picture the sea
we want to praise and adore you
because it makes us think
of your awesome and exciting power
and of the beauty of your peace.

Christ our Saviour,
when we picture the sea
we want to praise and adore you
for your power to calm the storms of life
and save us from the power of death.

Spirit of God,
when we picture the sea
we want to praise and adore you
for moving on the face of the waters
to bring order out of the chaos of existence.

We pray for those who make their livings
by sailing the world's oceans:
> to take cargo from one land to another;
> to carry traveller and tourist, soldier and
> aid-worker;
> to gather in the dwindling harvest of the sea.

We remember those who sail their boats for pleasure,
as recreation or to meet a personal challenge.
We pray too for ...
and for the lifeboat crews
who risk their lives to save others.

Loving God,
may they all be aware of your presence
as they sail your mighty oceans,
and may we too know you with us
on all our journeying through life.

AUGUST – Holidays

Reading: Exodus 23.10-12

God of the Sabbath,
we thank you for the freedoms of holiday time:
    freedom from work and routine;
    freedom to travel and have new experiences;
    freedom to rest and to play.
We thank you for the opportunities of holiday time:
    to view our lives from another angle;
    to spend time with family and friends;
    to be able to be ourselves.

We pray for all those going on holiday,
asking that they might enjoy themselves
and return relaxed and refreshed.

We pray for those worrying about their holiday,
afraid of things going wrong and spoiling it
or that tensions in relationships
will come to the surface.

We pray for those who dread the loneliness
when friends or family go away
and their normal social life is disrupted.

We pray for those diverse areas of the world
visited by tourists at this time,
asking that their people and resources
be treated with care and respect.

God of the Sabbath,
help us to make the most
of the freedoms of holiday time
to draw closer to one another and to you
to be re-created by the power of love.

SEPTEMBER – new start for the Church

Reading: Romans 12.1-5

Loving Creator, generous giver
of everything we need to live life in all its fullness,
we praise you for being a God of new beginnings
and thank you for the opportunities
this September brings.
Loving Saviour, our Way, our Truth, our Life,
who leads us and walks with us
into an unknown future,
we praise you for your costly offer of forgiveness
and thank you for calling us
to live new lives with you.
Loving Spirit, Breath of Life in our Church and world,
we praise you for the new gifts you pour on us
and thank you for binding us together
with the ties of love.

L: Lord, we offer ourselves to you:
R: Help us to know and to do your will.

Lord, in sorrowful confession we offer to you
our past shortcomings, failures and mistakes.
Help us to see them through your eyes, that, forgiven,
we may redeem our past
and press onwards to our goal.

L: Lord, we offer ourselves to you:
R: Help us to know and to do your will.

Lord, we pray for your world,
burdened by past mistakes,
asking your guidance
for those countries looking for change.
We pray for ....
We pray for your Church, struggling to become
a Church of the future, as well as of the past.
We pray for this church, for ....

And we pray for those who are afraid of what the
future may hold,
for those who are ill or whose loved ones are ill
and for those facing big changes in their lives.
We pray for ...

L: Lord, we offer ourselves to you:
R: Help us to know and to do your will.

Lord, this September,
we dedicate ourselves and our church to you.
Help us to rejoice
in the different gifts you have given us.
With the help of your Spirit,
we will use them wisely and well.
Together we will be Christ's body in the world today,
serving others with humility, enthusiasm and love.

L: Lord, we offer ourselves to you:
R: Help us to know and to do your will.

SEPTEMBER – New Educational Year
Reading: Proverbs 2.1-6

God our Teacher,
we hear the doors of school and college
being flung open once more
to welcome in children and students.
And we pray that the opening of those doors
may be the opening up of minds and lives
to knowledge, understanding and growth.

We pray for the youngest children
making their first steps on the journey of knowledge,
as they start school, for ...
and for those who face the challenge of a new school,
for ....
Lord, we know that sometimes school life
        can be hard,
but we pray that they may be upheld by you.
Help them to be interested in what they learn,
and to find enjoyment and support
in their friendships.

We pray for those going to college or university,
especially those leaving home for the first time, for ....
Be with them in the adventures of living and learning,
help them to grow, and realise their goals.

God our Teacher,
we pray for all who teach, at the start of this new year,
for ...
that they may take up their responsibilities
with renewed energy, enthusiasm and commitment.

We thank you, loving God,
source of wisdom, knowledge and understanding,
that you teach us the way, the truth and the life,
and encourage us as your disciples.
May we never stop learning about you,
and never stop sitting at your feet,
listening to your word.

SEPTEMBER – Racial Justice *(Week 38)*

Reading: Deuteronomy 10.17-19

All-knowing God,
we praise you for your justice.
You alone can see into our hearts and minds.
We are judged by the plumb-line of your love
and you teach us right from wrong:
we long for and demand justice for ourselves,
but sadly confess to you
the injustice that human beings show
     towards one another,
     towards people of different races.
We are horrified by the stories of injustice we hear
and mortified by some of the things
     done in your name.
Forgive us and help us to forgive one another.

L: We want to build a better future together;
R: A world like your kingdom
     of justice and love.

We bring to you the victims of racial injustice.
We pray for those treated as second-class citizens
because of their colour, accent or culture,
discriminated against in education or employment,
afforded scant respect, dignity or understanding.
We pray for the victims
     of violent hatred;
     of exploitation;
     of condescension.
Forgive us and help us to forgive one another.

L: We want to build a better future together;
R: A world like your kingdom
     of justice and love.

God of us all,
we want to be more like you;
not showing favour to some,
but generous and kind to all.
Search our hearts, loving God
and help us to root out our hidden prejudices,
so that our church, our society and our world
may be transformed by your justice.
Forgive us and help us to forgive one another.

L: We want to build a better future together;
**R: A world like your kingdom
of justice and love.**

SEPTEMBER/OCTOBER – Harvest

Reading: Deuteronomy 26.1-11

Creator God, we thank you
for giving to your creatures
such a splendid and diverse world,
with its rhythm of summer and winter,
springtime and harvest;
a world capable of feeding and sustaining all,
if only we would live as you want us to do.
We praise you for its beauty and generosity:
for its wonders that speak of your majesty and love,
and for the food you provide
for our needs and our enjoyment.

L: For all your loving gifts to us:
R: We praise and thank you.

Saviour God, we thank you
that you walk the earth around us like a sower,
flinging onto the soil of our lives
the seed of your gospel;
offering us new and productive lives in you
if we will open ourselves to respond to your call.
We praise you for the way in which you tend us,
showering us with love, forgiveness and faith,
warming us with your smile,
as you encourage us to grow.
We offer the first-fruits of our lives to you,
in our worship and our Christian living.

L: For all your loving gifts to us:
R: We praise and thank you.

Sustaining God, we thank you
for pouring the power of your life-giving Spirit
into the world, the Church, and into each one of us,
guiding us, uniting us and enriching all humankind.

We ask that the fruit of the Spirit in our lives
might be used to feed the hungry
of this hurting world.
May we show generosity to the poor and starving
and stand up for justice and freedom.
May we offer new life in you
to those who hunger for meaning,
and show your love
to those who are lonely or distressed.

L: For all your loving gifts to us:
R: We praise and thank you.

OCTOBER – Week of Prayer for World Peace *(Week 42)*

Reading: Isaiah 2.1-5

Have three candles ready to light.

Loving God, we long for peace
yet we often find it impossible to sustain.

We long for peace in our hearts and lives;
the peace your presence alone can bring.
But we are afraid to surrender ourselves to you,
to let go and fall back on your loving arms,
and discover the peace of trusting faith.

Light first candle.

We long for peace in our families,
in the communities in which we live,
and among the people with whom we work.
But everywhere there is suspicion and strife
and we find it hard to resist an argument.

Light second candle.

We long for peace in the world
and bring our heartfelt prayers for it to you.
We are wearied by the guilt and pain we feel
when news of war and conflict enters our homes;
sickened by the sight of corpses and injured children,
of lives ruined by loss and mutilating wounds.

Light third candle.

We long for that visionary time
when 'nation shall not lift sword against nation
neither shall they learn war any more'.
Help us to turn our longing prayers for peace
into lives committed to pursuing it.

Equip us to follow the Prince of Peace
on his long and painful journey to your kingdom
carrying the heavy cross of human sin.
We know that the path to peace is no easy way,
but slow, painstaking and costly.
We know that lasting peace will only come
when we seek justice and are prepared for sacrifice.
Loving God, with the power of your Spirit, guide us
to seek peace for ourselves,
our families and community,
to seek peace for your world.

OCTOBER – One World Week *(Week 43)*
Reading: Psalm 67

Loving God, we praise and worship you,
thankful that we can believe
that you hold the whole world in your hand
and that each one of us is as precious to you
as a child to its mother.

L: Let the peoples praise you, God:
R: Let all peoples praise you.

We are sorry, forgiving Creator,
that we do not see or treat others
as people who are important to you.
Looking at your world you must see
inhumanities of every kind;
we are ashamed and distressed.

L: Let the peoples praise you, God:
R: Let all peoples praise you.

In the name of Christ, who gave his life
to break down the barrier of sin,
help us to dedicate ourselves
to destroying the barriers humankind has made
that prevent the free flow of love
between your children.

L: Let the peoples praise you, God:
R: Let all peoples praise you.

When we are divided by racism or fear:
may the power of your love break through.
When we are divided by misunderstanding or
intolerance;
may the power of your love break through.
When there is division between rich and poor;
may the power of your love break through.

When there is division between
powerful and powerless;
may the power of your love break through.
The earth is yours, loving God;
and life belongs to you.

L: Let the peoples praise you, God:
R: Let all peoples praise you.

NOVEMBER – All Saints' Day (1 November)
Reading: Revelation 7.9-17

God of the living and the dead,
we praise and thank you
that we belong to that great multitude
which no one can count,
who worship, love and serve you.

We thank you for the first Christians,
who bravely took your gospel
to all kinds of people and places,
witnessing to the power of your love in their lives.
We thank you for their passion for your truth,
as they worked out what it meant to follow Christ,
and acted as midwives to the labours of your Spirit
at the birth of the infant Church.

We thank you for all who, through the ages,
have guarded and tended the lamp of faith,
keeping it burning through conflict and indifference.
We thank you for their commitment
that has brought the church to this present time.

And each of us, parent God, thanks you
for those who introduced us to the Way
and joined us on stretches of our journey of faith.
We remember, in silence, those who have died in you.

Silence

We rejoice that we belong to one community
on earth and in heaven.

May your Holy Spirit help us
to keep the flame of faith alive,
so that we, the saints of today,
may pass it on, burning brightly,
to the saints of tomorrow.

NOVEMBER – Remembrance Day
(11th November) *(Week 46)*
Reading: Revelation 22.1-5

So many young lives lost.
So many minds and bodies mutilated or scarred.
So many families torn apart.
So much destruction.

God of love and justice and peace,
on this Remembrance Day,
we remember the costs of war.

We remember the young men
who went so bravely, to fight
for their country or their cause
and gave up their lives.

We remember the families of those young men:
the heart-rending partings,
the anxious waiting for news,
the pain of loss.

We remember those who did not die
but came home damaged or haunted,
covering up their wounds,
unable to share their experiences,
sometimes ashamed of still being alive.

Loving God, we thank you
for all those who have made and still make sacrifices
out of a longing to make the world a better place.
We thank you for their bravery,
    their loyalty and
    their generosity.

May we never forget them,
but dedicate our lives to striving
for a just and peaceful world.

NOVEMBER Prisons Week *(Week 47)*

Reading: Matthew 25.31-46

God, our Teacher and our Saviour,
we thank you for opening our eyes
to Christ's presence in human lives,
in the need and pain of the world.

We confess to you that we have tried to ignore
the needs of the destitute, the stranger
    and the prisoner.
We have deafened our ears to your call
    coming from their lips.
Forgive us, as we would forgive others,
and give us the faith to see you
in the humanity of each individual
and the grace to love and care for them.

We pray for those prisoners
whose wrong turnings have brought them
to a place where they do not want to be.
We pray, too, for those so used to prison life
that they cannot cope with life outside.
Parent God, you made us for one another,
help us live together in respect and love.

We pray for those who work in prison
that they may respond to the human needs
of those for whom they are responsible.
May they not lose sight of their own humanity,
but find fulfilment in their job well done.
We pray for prison chaplains and visitors
offering concern, help and hope to those inside.

We pray for those leaving prison,
that they may be able to make a new start
and, by your grace, have the strength
to live within the laws of our society.

We pray that society might give them
the opportunities and support that they need.

We pray in the name of Jesus, who became human
that we might become more like you.

NOVEMBER – 'Children in Need'

Reading: Nehemiah 5.1-6

God, our father and our mother,
we thank you for the gift of children;
bringing love, with all its joys and demands,
   to their families,
hope and challenge to their communities,
and new life and insights to their church.

But as we pray, there come into our minds
the children of your world reaching out to us,
in need of our help, our love and our support.

Everywhere, if we can bear to look,
we see children living in poverty:
      some hungry, starving or malnourished,
      suffering the unnecessary diseases
      that come from lack of food and clean water;
      some unable to get medical care or an education;
      some exploited for their work or their bodies.
We pray for ....
We see children living in want:
      some unwanted, neglected or ignored,
      made to feel that they do not matter,
      and afraid that they will never amount to much;
      some physically, emotionally or sexually abused;
      many not knowing which way to turn.
We pray for ....
We see children fighting for their lives:
      some injured, sick or dying,
      struggling to cope with fear and pain;
      some with physical or mental disabilities,
      pushing at the restrictions imposed upon them;
      some bullied, rejected and depressed.
We pray for ....

They are all your children, loving God,
just as we rejoice to be;
all needing protection, compassion
and a better chance in life.
We pray for the work of charities
like 'Children in Need'
and for their many fund-raising efforts.
God of justice, give us the will and strength
to give your children what they need to live fully.

NOVEMBER – Youth in the Church *(Week 48)*
Reading 1 Timothy 4.12-16

Let us praise the God of Abraham, Isaac and Jacob,
the God of youth, of middle- and old-age.

We are sorry, God, parent of us all,
that we do not always listen with respect
to the voices of the different generations
of your people.

Because our world is changing so quickly,
the insights and wisdom of the mature
are often ignored.

L: Forgive us:
R: And help us.

Because your Church is weary
and suspicious of change
the words and ideas of the young are often dismissed.
L: Forgive us:
R: And help us.

We pray for, and with, the youth of the Church,
who are on the early stretches of faith's journey,
asking that nothing distract them from their goal
of loving, trusting and following your Son, Jesus.
May your Spirit strengthen them
to resist those pressures of our society
that would pull them away from you.
May your Spirit excite and challenge them
with a sense of purpose and fresh opportunities
making them feel fully alive.
May your Spirit fill them with hope and joy,
pointing them to a bright future
as your followers, workers and friends.

Teach your Church, loving God,
to value its young people:
    their energy, new visions and enthusiasm;
    their commitment to you and to one another.
May we all find encouragement,
as together we seek your will for your Church
    and for your world;
as together we seek to obey
    your commandments to love.

NOVEMBER/DECEMBER – Advent

Reading: Isaiah 52.7-10

In the long dark days of winter,
the cold and dismal days of waiting for the spring,
you surprise us into life,
by the joy of your good news, loving God.
You come as the king of the world.
You come as our deliverer.

Forgive us when we are not prepared for you!

Open our eyes, Creator God,
to see your presence within our lives;
to see:

> the good being done all around us;
> the relationships that are loving and supportive;
> the challenges to human indifference.

Open our ears, Word of life,
to hear your message of salvation;
to hear:

> the offer of a new, full life in you;
> the call to follow you as your disciples;
> your encouragement as we walk the way
>   of self-giving love.

Open our hearts, Spirit of God,
to receive your power within us;
to receive:

> your gifts of hope and joy and peace;
> the love that binds us together;
> the courage to witness to your good news.

You are coming, Saviour God.
Help us to be ready for you, alert and prepared
to see and hear and serve you
this Christmas and every day of our lives.

DECEMBER – World AIDS Day (1 December)
Reading: Mark 1.29-34, 40-44

Loving God, we find disease hard to bear
and even harder to accept and understand.
Why is it that the freedom of your creation
involves so much suffering for your children?

But we want to thank you for offering us hope,
for, in Christ, we have seen your presence
with those who are sick.
We have witnessed his anger at their suffering
and so had our own anger understood and affirmed.
We have witnessed his reaching out to the sick,
his willingness to touch the untouchable,
to heal them and draw them back
into their living community,
and have heard your call to us to do the same.

We pray for those with AIDS, throughout our world,
and those with lives poisoned by HIV.
We pray for the young people
whose lives will be cut short
and the children made orphans
and themselves unwell.
Rich and poor, black and white, straight and gay,
we think with anger of the multitude of lives
ruined by this merciless disease,
and of the ignorance, prejudice and fear that
surround it.
We bring to you our sorrow at the isolation of the sick
who suffer loneliness and condemnation
as well as illness
and the fear of coming pain and death.

Gracious God, we thank you
that so many have poured so much
into trying to help.
We thank you for the discovery of better treatments
and for the loving humanity shown to many sufferers.
We pray, God of justice, that in the same way
that this disease has not been selective in its victims,
neither will we be in its treatment.
Show us how we can help
to bring your touch to the victims of AIDS.

DECEMBER – International Day of Disabled Persons (3 December)

Reading: 2 Corinthians 12.7b-12

Understanding God, you know how it is
to be unable to do all you would like
because you have chosen not to force us
    to love and obey you.
You know because you are disabled by our freedom,
and your work is dependent
on our responding to you in love.

And so we bring to you the frustrations
of our own individual limitations.
Use or transform them, enabling God,
that we, your people, may serve your suffering world.

On this day we remember in our prayers
the challenges faced by those living with disabilities
caused by accident of birth or accident in life:
        the challenge to have their personhood
           recognised;
        the challenge to get equal rights;
        the challenge to reach their potential;
        the challenge to know fulfilment in their lives.

God of change, we thank you
for all the progress that has been made
in understanding the needs that disability brings
and the loss that society sustains
when these needs are not met.
We are sorry that there is still so far to go
until equal rights and status are achieved.

We praise and thank you
    for all who have campaigned hard
    for those rights;
    for all whose work and caring involves
    being alongside those with disabilities.

We pray for ....

Together may we strive to transform this world
into your kingdom of justice, joy and love.

DECEMBER – Christmas

Reading: Luke 2.1-7 or Luke 2.1-20

All-seeing and all-knowing God,
the source of all life and love,
we worship you this Christmas,
for coming to us in Jesus as a helpless child
so that we might see and know you.

We thank you, generous God,
for offering us the gift of life in all its fullness
in Christ's birth and loving ministry,
and in his death and resurrection.

In prayer we offer to you
our mixed feelings at Christmastime:
     our happiness and our sadness;
     our sometimes weary excitement;
     our anxious searching for Christmas joy.

Forgive us when we lose sight
of the generosity of your Christmas love,
and help us to accept it graciously
so that we may find your true peace again.

We pray to you, Immanuel, God with us,
because you came to us as a child in need
and still meet us in the needs of others.

We bring to you in prayer
the suffering of the people of your world,
praying for ...
and the suffering of those whom we know
who are ill ...
or who have been bereaved ....

We remember those who are lonely or anxious,
and all who will find this Christmas difficult.
Help us to show your Christmas love to your world,
to tell of your good news for all humankind.

Prayers for Various Occasions

ACHIEVEMENTS

Reading: 1 Corinthians 9.24-27

Start by sharing news and details of the achievements (academic, sporting, charitable, etc.) being celebrated.

God, who challenges us
to be and do our very best for you,
we thank you that ... *(name/s)*
took up the challenge of ... and achieved ....
Help us all to listen out
for the challenges you set us in our daily lives.

L: Companion God:
R: Help us to respond to the challenges you set before us.

God, who encourages us
to persevere in our worthwhile endeavours
we thank you for those who supported *(name/s)*
for ....
Help us all to focus our lives
on achieving the things you ask us to do
and to offer support and encouragement
to one another.

L: Companion God:
R: Help us to respond to the challenges you set before us.

God, who forgives us
our failures and half-heartedness,
while we rejoice at the achievement of ... *(name/s)*

we also need to confess to you
the times we have set our sights
on the wrong goals ...
and the times when we have too easily given up
our struggles to follow you.

L: Companion God:
**R: Help us to respond to the challenges you
     set before us.**

God, who rejoices with us
at our achievements and growth,
we pray that you will continue to bless
... *(name/s)* as they ...
and that you will bless our lives, too,
as we try to follow Jesus
along the path of self-giving love.

L: Companion God:
**R: Help us to respond to the challenges you
     set before us.**

ANIMALS

Reading: Matthew 18.12-14

Creator God,
the story of the lost sheep
and the conscientious shepherd
reminds us of your love for us
and our need and love for you;
it reminds us that you ask us to care
for the creatures you have entrusted to us.

We are filled with wonder
when we look at them,
from microscopic organism to giant whale.
We praise you for all we can learn from them,
    as we see their design, beauty and variety;
    as we study their forms and behaviour;
    as we observe how they change and adapt
    to different environments and conditions.

We thank you
for the animals and birds of field and farm
who supply our needs *(we pray for ...).*
We thank you
for animals who help and work alongside us
(we pray for ...).
We thank you
for the companionship of animals;
for the love and comfort of our pets
and the pleasure and sense of peace
we receive from them.
We remember in our prayers
those saddened by the loss of a beloved pet
(we pray for ...).
May they find comfort, loving God,
in remembering their friendship
with gratitude and joy.
We want to say sorry

for our misuse and exploitation of animals
and for the cruelty they sometimes suffer.
Help us to see them and their needs
as you want us to see them.
Help us to accept our responsibilities
to care for and protect them,
for we know that even sparrows
are watched over by you.
Creator God, thank you for animals.

ANNIVERSARY – Church

Reading: Ephesians 3.14-21

God of past, present and future,
we come with joy to pray to you
as we celebrate the anniversary of this church
and its life and witness through the years.

L: Glory to Christ in your church:
R: Today and for evermore!

God of our past,
we thank you for the founding fathers and mothers
who responded to your call to establish this church.
We thank you for all its faithful people
who have worked and prayed
and given themselves, out of love for you,
to those both within and outside these walls.

L: Glory to Christ in your church:
R: Today and for evermore!

God of the present,
we thank you for your unfailing love
that encourages, inspires and enables us
to continue sharing the good news of Christ
with one another and with our neighbours.
We pray for those of this church and community
who are ill, anxious or sorrowful, for....
We ask that our hearts may be open to your presence
and our ears may be tuned to your call.

L: Glory to Christ in your church:
R: Today and for evermore!

God of the future,
we do not know what lies ahead,
but we hear you challenging us
to walk with you and with one another,
without fear, into the unknown future.
Forgive us our past mistakes and failings,
and clear our vision to see the way ahead.

L: Glory to Christ in your church:
R: Today and for evermore!

ANNIVERSARY – Sunday School/Junior Church

Reading: Mark 10.13-16

Sing together two hymns/songs, one old and one modern, suitable for young people.

Loving God,
we thank you that your word tells us
that your kingdom belongs
to those who are still growing.

We thank you for the life of our Sunday
School/Junior Church
which has welcomed and still welcomes
growing youngsters with open arms.
We thank you for its willingness to share with them
the reality of the spiritual life;
the life, death and resurrection of Jesus
and the stories he told;
the gospel of forgiving love;
the offer of real life in you,
and the witness of your Church.

We thank you for the many children
for whom the Sunday School/Junior Church
has been the starting place
for their life-long Christian pilgrimage.
In silence we think about
what the early Christian teaching we received
means to us ....

Silence

We pray for teachers and young people
as they explore together
what it means to follow Christ today;

and as they experience
the joys and challenges of faith and life
in our changing, complex,
    and sometimes hostile world.

We pray that,
with the help and guidance of your Spirit,
our church may be a place
where children not only feel wanted
but where they want to be.
Make us all, young and old, one living community
united in love and praise for you,
growing into the people you want us to be.

ANNIVERSARY – Wedding

Reading: 1 Corinthians 13.1-13

*Make a small display of wedding and family photos
and other mementoes, etc.
Sing together a hymn sung at the wedding.*

God of love and life,
we praise and thank you
for giving us one another to love.
We thank you for the marriage of ... *(names)*
who together took a decisive step
on the adventurous journey of loving
at their wedding ... years ago.

God among us,
we thank you that we can share their joy at this time
as they celebrate a love that has lasted the years.
We thank you for the happiness, security and support
that love has brought to them and their family.

God of challenge and change,
we thank you for the love that grows within marriage:
> developing in new ways
> as husband and wife mature;
> enduring sorrows and adversities together;
> learning to forgive, forgo and rebuild;
> discovering new delights in one another.

God of everlasting love,
your commandment to love one another
is the hardest thing you ask of us,
and so we confess our failings in loving.

Silence

We thank you that you give us:
>   your forgiveness in Christ;
>   the grace to persevere;
>   the help of your Holy Spirit in our lives;
>   and the rewards of joy and peace.

We pray for ... *(names of couple)*
and for their family ... *(names of children and grandchildren)*
and especially for ... *(any special concern)*.
May the love that they share
strengthen and shape their lives
and be a blessing to many,
today and in the years to come.

BIBLE STUDY

Reading: Acts 8.26-38

Hold the Bibles open at the passage that is to be studied.

L: Loving God, speak to us as we read and study the Bible:
R: **Draw us closer to you.**

Sometimes we are puzzled
by what we find in the Bible.
So much of it is hard to understand or to accept.
Spirit of God, clear our minds
and give us the courage and determination
    to struggle together
    to wrest a meaning from its words.

L: Loving God, speak to us as we read and study the Bible:
R: **Draw us closer to you.**

Sometimes we approach the Bible with fixed ideas,
We tend to take from it
only what agrees with our beliefs.
Spirit of God, clear our minds
and give us the faith and humility
    to share together
    new and challenging discoveries.

L: Loving God, speak to us as we read and study the Bible:
R: **Draw us closer to you.**

Sometimes we approach the Bible
burdened by our own ignorance.
Reading it can make us feel anxious or embarrassed.
Spirit of God, clear our minds

and give us the trust and openness
to confess together
our need for help in understanding.

L: Loving God, speak to us as we read and study the
Bible:
R: Draw us closer to you.

Sometimes we approach the Bible
with joyful curiosity.
We are eager to learn more about you.
Spirit of God, clear our minds
and give us the grace and love
to listen to one another
as we share insights and experiences.

L: Loving God, speak to us as we read and study the
Bible:
R: Draw us closer to you.

BIRTH

Reading: Psalm 22.9-10

God our Father and our Mother,
we offer you thankful prayers,
with hearts leaping with joy and excitement
at the news of the birth of ... *(name of baby)*.

God of Love,
     you were there at her/his conception.
God of Patience,
     you were with her/his family as they waited.
God of Strength,
     you were there at the labour and the birth.
God our Father and our Mother,
     each of us belongs to you.

We ask your blessing on this baby
as s/he sets out on the journey of life
in a world fraught with dangers and difficulties.
We know that you will watch over and guide her/him
and uphold her/him with your love.

We ask your blessing on ... *(names of parents)*.
Give them all the love, wisdom
and patience they will need
in the care and nurture of ... *(name of baby)*.
We pray for ... *(names of baby's brother/s and/or
sister/s)*
as they welcome this baby into their family
and adjust to the new life together.

(We thank you for ... [name of baby]
but we also want to pray for ... [name any special
concern]
asking that they may know your presence with them
and feel the strengthening touch of your hand.)

God our Father and our Mother,
accept our prayer of grateful thanks
for the miracle of birth:
for the coming of a child
who brings joy and hope to a sad and tired world
and who brings new love into our lives.

BIRTHDAYS

Reading: Psalm 139.1-6, 13-18

Loving God, we praise you
for all that you have done for us:
for the beauty and generosity of your creation;
for your offers of forgiveness and never-ending love;
for your presence with us throughout our lives.

L: Faithful God, we praise you:
R: For the wonder of your love for us.

We thank you that we can believe
that each one of us is special to you:
for you sent your Son Jesus Christ
to live among us and to die for us;
you raised him to victory over sin and death
so that we might know the power of your goodness
and accept your invitation to give our lives to you.

L: Faithful God, we praise you:
R: For the wonder of your love for us.

We know that ... *(name of birthday person)*
is special to you
and, as we celebrate her/his *(number)*th birthday,
we thank you for her/him.
We thank you for all that s/he means to us
and to those who are close to her/him ....
We thank you that s/he
is able to celebrate this birthday
and, most of all, we thank you
that you are there in the story of her/his life.

L: Faithful God, we praise you:
R: For the wonder of your love for us.

Loving God, we ask your blessing on us all.
We pray that in the unknown years to come
we may feel you upholding us
through any sorrow or weakness
and know you as our constant companion.
Give us the grace to continue witnessing
to the power of your love in our lives.

L: Faithful God, we praise you:
R: For the wonder of your love for us.

BUILDING PROJECT

Reading: Ezra 3.10-13

Let us come to God
whose wisdom is beyond our human knowledge
for the help that we need with our building project.

Loving God,
we thank you for your challenge
to alter the fabric of this church
to make it more suitable
for worshipping and serving you in this present age.

We confess our doubts and worries
about the task we are undertaking.
We confess that we feel daunted
when it seems we have more questions than answers:
 questions about time and money;
 questions about Christian priorities;
 questions about the will of the congregation;
 and questions about the needs of the community.
We look to you in prayer,
to help us to find answers.

Creator God,
we want to make something worthy of you.
Saviour God,
we want this project to be good news.
Spirit of God,
we want this project to draw us closer to one another.

God with us,
help us to feel our way forward prayerfully.
Help us to think through the issues with great care
in the light of our knowledge of your loving purposes.
Give us a new vision for this building
and strengthen us
with the courage and faith we need to pursue it.

Loving God,
take this building and use it
for the glory of your kingdom.

CARE HOMES FOR THE ELDERLY
Reading: Psalm 23

God, our loving Shepherd,
wherever we go, you are there,
whatever we experience, you are with us.
We know that we can trust your promise
that you will be with us until the end of time.

We pray for the elderly who are on the home stretch
of their life's journey.

L: In your love and mercy:
R: **Hear our prayer.**

We rejoice with those who know happiness,
who feel content and valued;
blessed with an uplifting faith,
with loving friends and family.

We ask your help for those who are sad,
finding the last haul a difficult struggle;
burdened with ill-health
with loneliness or anxiety.

L: In your love and mercy:
R: **Hear our prayer.**

We pray for the work of residential homes
who offer care to the aged,
asking that they may lovingly seeking to meet
the physical, emotional and spiritual needs
of those entrusted to their care.
We pray for ...*(local homes and residents etc.)*

L: In your love and mercy:
R: **Hear our prayer.**

May we, by our interest, involvement and prayers,
offer carers support in their work
within the homes and the wider community.

Loving Shepherd, may your goodness
follow us all the days of our lives,
that we may dwell in your house for ever.

L: In your love and mercy:
R: Hear our prayer.

CHILDREN'S CLUBS OR PROJECTS – PREPARATION

Reading: Matthew 7.24-27

This prayer could be shared out between different leaders.

God of meaning and purpose,
it is knowing you and your steadfast love
that makes us glad to be alive.

Help us to share the joys of faith
with those starting out on the journey of life,
as we introduce them to the riches of your gospel.

We long to help them see
that they too can discover what life is about
if they put their faith in you.

We are all your children, loving God,
and you treasure the childlike.
Help us as we learn and grow together.

We want to hear laughter, God of happiness,
and see transforming smiles
as our hearts dance
to the rhythm of your joy.

We want to express ourselves, Creator God,
and know the glow of achievement,
as we learn to make
something beautiful or new.

We want to discover friendship, loving God,
as we share this experience together,
as we get to know new people
and try to help one another.

We need to feel Jesus with us
radiating his love for children
through what is done and said
by his faithful followers.

It is in his name that we pray
and ask for a blessing on this ....

CHURCH CONFERENCE/SYNOD

Reading: Romans 12.6-18

Creator God, we praise and adore you
    for speaking into being all that is;
    for giving us this world and one another;
    for making our hearts restless
        until we find you.
Saviour God, we praise and adore you
    for sharing our human life with us;
    for experiencing its frustrations;
        its vulnerability and longings;
    for redeeming it with your undying love.
Spirit of God, we praise and adore you
    for the power of your transforming presence
    in the world, the Church and our lives;
    for your gifts of wisdom
        of courage, joy and peace
    and of the love that unites us.
Creator, Saviour and Holy Spirit,
we praise and adore you.

Silence

Confident of your forgiveness and healing power
we open our hearts to you as we confess our failures
to be the people you want us to be:
    our lack of love and understanding;
    of wisdom and vision;
    of commitment to your gospel.

Silence

We pray for the ... *conference* at ...
asking you to open ears and minds and hearts
to your word for your Church at this time.

Silence

We pray especially for the discussions about ...
and for the people and the situations
that are causing us concern ....

Silence

We pray for your Church
that we may remain faithful and obedient to you
in all the challenges and complexities
of this present age.

Silence

Holy God, set us alight with your Spirit,
that we may shine as a beacon,
offering hope and direction
to those lost in darkness and confusion.
May this *conference* show us how we can share
your good news with our needy world.

CHURCH MEETING

Reading: 1 Corinthians 1.1-9

Constant God,
we thank you for keeping faith with us,
so that however busy we are,
through all the ups and downs of church life,
we can know that you are our God
and we are your people.
Saviour God,
we thank you for calling us
to share in the life of your Son, Jesus Christ.
We dedicate ourselves,
all that we are, say and do,
to witness to his gospel of love.
Spirit of God,
we thank you for the many gifts
you have bestowed on the people of this church.
Help us to use them wisely
and to share them freely.
We ask for a vision for our future
and that you might draw us closer together in love.

L: In your love and mercy:
R: Hear our prayer.

Wise and loving God, make us fully aware
of your presence with us in this *meeting*:
help us to hear you in what is said;
      to feel you in the love that shapes our thinking;
      to find you in the decisions that we make.
We ask for your help as we discuss ....

L: In your love and mercy:
R: Hear our prayer.

We bring to you in prayer
members of this meeting who cannot be with us ....

L: In your love and mercy:
R: Hear our prayer.

May this church and congregation
be a revelation of you to those whose lives they touch.
May it be a holy place where the seeker can find you
and experience the truth, love and comfort
        of your eternal saving power.

CLOSING SESSION OF FELLOWSHIP MEETING etc.

Reading: Philippians 4.4-9

God the First and the Last,
we praise you for your faithful love for us
throughout our lives.

L: We praise you for all that is past:
R: And trust you for all that's to come.

We thank you for the fellowship of this group:
for the deepening of friendships;
for the mutual help and support;
for the fun we enjoy together.

L: We praise you for all that is past:
R: And trust you for all that's to come.

We thank you for the good times we have:
for the worship we offer together;
for learning about new things;
for meals and refreshments we share.

L: We praise you for all that is past:
R: And trust you for all that's to come.

We thank you for helping us through the bad times:
when there has been a death ... *(we pray for ...)*
when there is injury or illness ... *(we pray for ...)*
when there is anger, disagreement or hurt.

L: We praise you for all that is past:
R: And trust you for all that's to come.

Loving God,
we will miss these times together.
We think of them with gratitude and joy
and look forward to being with each other
in the future.

L: We praise you for all that is past:
R: And trust you for all that's to come.

COMMUNITY

Reading: Luke 4.14-20

Display a simple map or pictures of the area.
Adapt the prayer to the particular community.

Loving God, we praise you
because you have good news for all humankind.
Through your Son, Jesus Christ, you offer:
>   freedom from sin, guilt and despair;
>   life in all its fullness;
>   the healing and restoring power of love.

When we look at the community here in ...
we confess that,
although we know that you want us to be
the Body of Christ in this place,
we rarely live up to that challenge.
We confess our lack of:
>   vision and determination;
>   energy and commitment;
>   imagination and self-giving love.
Too often we just want to shut the church doors
and get on with the things
that make us feel comfortable,
caring for our own spiritual and emotional needs.
Saving God, forgive us and redirect us.

We think about the streets we live in
and travel through,
picturing where the people of this community live:
some of them satisfied with themselves
and their lives,
but others looking for something else,
feeling that their deeper needs go unmet.
We think about the schools ...
and the children and young people of this area.

We think about the health centres ...
those who work in them,
and those who are ill or infirm.
We think about the shops and businesses ...
the places for leisure ...
and the other churches and places of worship ....
We think about our neighbours
and pray for the work we are doing with ....

Spirit of God, come to us in our thinking
and tell us what more we should be doing
to serve this community that you love.

CONCERT etc.

Reading: Psalm 98

Creator God, we thank you for the gift of music:
    touching our hearts with joy;
    stirring up our deepest emotions;
    feeding our spirits
    and expressing things we cannot say.

L: God of music, for the song you put into our
      hearts:
R: We praise and thank you.

We thank you that we can be here *today/tonight*
to listen to ....
As we listen, draw close to us
so that our souls may feel the beat of your love.

L: God of music, for the song you put into our
      hearts:
R: We praise and thank you.

We thank you for musical talents
and for the hard work and dedication
of those who practise to improve their skills
as they prepare them to share with others.

L: God of music, for the song you put into our
      hearts:
R: We praise and thank you.

We pray for the music makers:
    for composers, orchestras and conductors;
    for soloists, choirs and bands.
May they find joy and fulfilment in what they do.

L: God of music, for the song you put into our
      hearts:
R: We praise and thank you.

Life-giving God, when we worship you
your Spirit comes to us in the music that we share.
Help us to perform our Christian living
in harmony with the music of your gospel love.

L: God of music, for the song you put into our
    hearts:
R: We praise and thank you.

CRIME – against an individual

Reading: Psalm 17.6-9

Loving God, we want to praise you
by becoming the people you mean us to be
as we work for the coming of your kingdom.
But then something like this happens.

And the reality of evil, greed and selfishness
leaves us feeling shaken, unsafe and confused.
We wonder whether our attempts at goodness
will ever counterbalance
the weight of wickedness in our world.
We realise again how much we all need
your saving love.

We come to you to pray for ... *(name/s)*
asking that you will give *him/her/them*
the knowledge of your presence
to comfort, calm and strengthen them.
We pray that ....
Guide us by your Holy Spirit
to find the right ways to help them.

Silence

Sometimes we find such situations
so difficult to understand
that we do not know what to think
or how to shape our prayers;
but we make our prayers knowing
that you understand everything.

You gaze into every heart and mind,
and see the dark things growing there.
You sorrow alongside us
at the destruction that they cause.

And in Jesus you knew what it is to be
a victim of hatred and evil
and what it is to feel
the fear of violence and loss.

Loving God, whatever life throws at us,
you promise to be in it with us
and that a faith in your victorious love
will bring our souls safely through.

CRIME – against the church
Reading: Psalm 37.1-9

All-knowing God, you understand how we feel
about what has happened to this church.
We feel upset, angry and let down.

L: O Lord, our Strength and our Redeemer:
R: Help us to trust in you and do good.

Forgiving God, we confess to you
our shock and bitterness
at the spoiling of this place of worship;
where we offer prayers and praise to you
and love and understanding to one another.

L: O Lord, our Strength and our Redeemer:
R: Help us to trust in you and do good.

We are afraid that our angry feelings
towards those who have done this
may not be acceptable to you.
May your Holy Spirit free us from our resentment
and help us to see what has happened as you see it.

L: O Lord, our Strength and our Redeemer:
R: Help us to trust in you and do good.

Challenging God,
help us to remember
that this church building does not belong to us,
but to you,
and that in Jesus we know you as a God
who brings good out of evil.

L: O Lord, our Strength and our Redeemer:
R: Help us to trust in you and do good.

Restoring God,
we pray for those working hard
to repair/clean up this church, for ....
We pray, too, for the perpetrators of this crime,
that you will reach out to touch them,
to repair and clean their hearts and lives.

L: O Lord, our Strength and our Redeemer:
R: Help us to trust in you and do good.

DEATH

Reading: 1 Corinthians 15.50-58

We feel sad today, listening God,
because of the death of ... *(name)*, our sister/brother.
We know we will not see them again in this life
and that they will be missed by
their family and friends.

We praise and thank you, eternal God,
that in Christ you have offered us the reassurance
that death is not the end of who we are
nor the extinguishing of all our hopes.

You understand that for many of us
the thought of our own death is a frightening one
that we try to push to the back of our minds.
We do not allow its reality
to be an important factor in the way we live
and see our lives.
Forgive us our lack of faith in you
and help us to come to terms with our mortality.

We remember the life of our sister/brother ... *(name)*,
and thank you for them:
 for all that they have meant to us;
 for the love that they have shown
 and the good things that they did ...
 for ...
 for their faith in you.

Silence

We pray for those who mourn them, for ... *(names)*,
asking that they may feel you close to them now,
 comforting them as they suffer
 and enfolding them in your loving arms.

Silence

Thank you, mighty God,
for giving us the victory
through your Son Jesus Christ,
    who freely gave his life for us on the cross
    and was raised to life again
    so that we might know
    that nothing can separate us from your love.

DISASTER – natural

Reading: Psalm 46.1-7

Creator God,
we want to offer you our praise
but when we try to picture your creation
instead of wondering at its beauty
we are appalled at sights of the death and destruction
caused by the ... *(disaster)* in ... *(place)*.

Silence

Horrific images are seared into our minds,
causing us to wonder
at the cruelty and ugliness in parts of your creation;
causing us to question its goodness.

L: God, our refuge and our stronghold:
R: Be our help in times of trouble.

Saviour God,
in your Son, Jesus Christ,
you reached out to those who suffered,
restoring them with your loving touch;
in your incarnation you knew the suffering
of loss and pain and death.
We pray for the people of ... *(place)*,
knowing that you suffer in this disaster with them
and reach out to them
in every loving and healing touch.

Silence

L: God, our refuge and our stronghold:
R: Be our help in times of trouble.

Spirit of God,
your presence in our lives
inspires us to love and serve one another
and gives us hope for the future.
We pray for all those who are working
to rescue the people of ... *(place)*,
to provide them with food and shelter,
with medicine and comfort ....

Silence

We pray for the survivors
that they may be able to rebuild their lives
and look to the future.

L: God, our refuge and our stronghold:
R: Be our help in times of trouble.

DISASTER – accidents, attacks or atrocities etc.

Reading: Jonah 2.2-7

God of our lives, we bring to you
our horror, shock and anger
at the news of the ... *(disaster)*

Silence

L: Listening God, in our distress:
R: We call to you.

God of our lives, we bring to you
the victims of this disaster;
we remember those who have died ....

Silence

Compassionate God, you love them
and know them all by name.

L: Listening God, in our distress:
R: We call to you.

We pray for those who have survived
but are physically or mentally scarred ....

Silence

Saving God, may they experience healing
and come to find peace.

L: Listening God, in our distress:
R: We call to you.

God of our lives, we bring to you
those who have been bereaved ...
and their feelings of loss and despair.

Silence

Loving Shepherd, be with all who walk
in the valley of the shadow of death.

L: Listening God, in our distress:
R: We call to you.

God of our lives, we bring to you
those called on to go and help
in the aftermath of this disaster ....

Silence

Restoring God, may they find release
from the trauma of flashbacks and feelings of regret.

L: Listening God, in our distress:
R: We call to you.

God of our lives, we bring to you
the consequences of this disaster for all of us;
asking that something new and good
might come from it
to make our world a safer, more caring place.

L: Listening God, in our distress:
R: We call to you.

DISMISSAL PRAYERS

Go out in the name of God
to love and care for God's creation.
Go out in the name of Christ
to share the good news of salvation.
Go out in the power of the Holy Spirit
to share the riches of life in God.

Lit up by the love of God,
we go to shine hope and joy
in the dark places of our world.

Wherever we go, God goes with us.
Whatever we do, God is beside us.
Whatever happens to us, God will uphold us.
May we always be aware of God's presence.

Go out into the world as followers of Jesus,
putting all your trust in God.
At every step keep God in mind
and the Spirit will direct your path.

God the Creator loves you;
go with courage.
God in Christ has saved you;
go with joy.
God the Spirit lives in you;
go in peace.

Take the love of this place with you
to warm the lives of those you meet, in God's name.
Take the friendship of this place with you
to reach out to the lonely, in Christ's name.
Take the prayers of this place with you
to bless others with the peace of God's Spirit.

The blessing of the God of love
encircle each one of us
now and for evermore.

DIVORCE or the ending of a relationship
Reading: Psalm 89.1, 2

Faithful God,
we love and adore you
>   because your love for us is never-ending;
>   because in Christ you gave everything
>   to bring us back to you;
>   because your Holy Spirit fills our lives
>   with faith and hope and peace.

We acknowledge, with sorrow,
that our love for you is weak and flickering
compared with the strength and constancy
of your love for us.
We confess that our relationships
fall short of your vision for our lives.

Silence

We bring to you our sorrow and concern
at hearing of the ... *(break up)*
of ... *(names).*

Silence

May they feel your presence with them
as they struggle with their pain and loss.
May you guide them in their decision-making
and touch them to comfort and heal.

Silence

We pray for the families and friends of ... *(names)*
(and especially for ... *[name/s]*)

Silence

You know what they are feeling and thinking;
you understand their anger, grief and bewilderment,
(or other);
their fear of what the future might hold.
We pray that in their need they might know
the care and support of your loving people.

Silence

God of our lives,
we cannot know what the future holds for ... *(names)*
but we can hear you calling us all on
to walk with you into the new.

DRAMA

Reading: Job 38.1-11
or another dramatic reading

Creator God, we worship and praise you
for speaking into being such a dramatic world:
>   full of noise – thunder crashing and waves
>   roaring;
>   full of light – the flash of lightning and
>   reflections of the sun;
>   full of movement – rushing wind
>   and falling rain;
>   full of beauty – the sunset, the rainbow,
>   the lilies of the field.
We thank you for this world
of excitement and wonder;
a world that points us to you.

Saviour God, we worship and praise you,
for you are the supreme story-teller,
pointing us to truths about ourselves and you.
In Jesus you spoke to us in parables
that stir up our minds and hearts
and encourage us to respond to your love.

Spirit of God, we worship and praise you
for inspiring us to explore and express ourselves
through music and dance, drama and writing,
art, poetry and acts of worship.
You move us, enlighten us and delight us,
making our lives dance to your rhythm.
You gift us laughter and joy.

We thank you for this ... *(performance)*;
for its original conception and design
and for all the preparation
that is going/has gone into it.

You, God of every present moment, are/were there:
in the hard work and flashes of inspiration;
in the companionship and co-operation;
in the frustrations and the laughter.

We think of the people we are/will be missing,
unable to be on stage or in the audience
because of *ill health or ...*
We pray for ....

God of our lives, we worship and praise you
for your gift of drama
and for all our dramatic glimpses of you.

ECUMENICAL SERVICES or meetings

Reading: Galatians 3.26-29

The paragraphs of this prayer could be read by representatives from the different churches.

God our Maker, we worship and praise you.
You spoke creation into being
and fashioned humankind, male and female,
in your own image.
You did not design us to be alone
but so that we can love and serve you together
and meet you in one another.

L: We are the family of God:
R: Made one in Christ Jesus, our brother.

God our Saviour, we worship and praise you.
When we had turned our backs on you,
going our own ways and not yours,
you did not leave us lost and afraid
but came alongside us in Christ,
turning us around with your offer of forgiveness,
lovingly leading us along the path to life.

L: We are the family of God:
R: Made one in Christ Jesus, our brother.

God our Inspirer, we worship and praise you.
The transforming power of your love sweeps
into our life together,
blowing away our fears and prejudices.
You give us the strength and enthusiasm we need
to live together as the body of Christ,
loving and serving your world.

L: We are the family of God:
R: Made one in Christ Jesus, our brother.

We pray for the people among whom we live and worship,
especially for ... *(any special need).*

L: Loving God, in your mercy
R: Hear our prayer.

We pray for the Church, both here and throughout the world,
especially for ... *(any special problems or projects).*

L: Loving God, in your mercy:
R: Hear our prayer.

We pray for our work and witness together,
especially for ... *(any special shared project).*

Listening God, you hear our prayers, for

L: We are the family of God:
R: Made one in Christ Jesus, our brother.

ELECTIONS

Reading: Isaiah 11.1-5

Display a variety of election pamphlets and posters, newspaper articles etc.

Sovereign and all-knowing God,
we pray that we may be given wisdom,
vision and compassion
as we consider our votes in this election.
We pray that those who seek to represent us
may be guided by wisdom, vision and compassion
as they consider their policies and aims.

God of goodness and faithfulness,
the media constantly bombard us
with bad news about your world,
in crowing exposés, fatalistic observations
and cynical comments.
We feel tempted to walk the easy path
of apathy, cynicism and comfortable ignorance.
Forgive us, loving God, and restore us.
Remind us again of the good news of Jesus
who, by his life and teaching, death and resurrection,
offers hope and fullness of life to humankind
and challenges us to set our feet
on the difficult path to your kingdom.

God of holiness and justice,
we pray for those looking to be elected
to *national/local* government at this time.
(We pray for ... [name/s]).
May your Holy Spirit give them
the gifts and skills they need
and fill them with integrity,
understanding and compassion.
May they commit themselves to serve us faithfully
and to improve the quality of life for those in need.

God of our lives,
in the Bible you grant us beautiful visions
of the kind of governments
you want for your world.
Help us not to be selfish in our voting
but to consider prayerfully
how we should honour you with our decisions.

ENJOYING CREATION

Reading: Matthew 6.25-34

Make a small arrangement of natural objects or put up a few pictures.

Creator God, we praise and thank you
for the ways in which we experience you
through the sights and sounds,
the feel, smell and taste,
of the world around us.

We rejoice at the way in which
the beauty of the world
can make us feel close to you.
We recall times in our lives
when you have met us in its beauty ....

Silence

Thank you, loving Maker, for this special gift.

We rejoice at the way in which
the life of plants and animals
help us to trust in your love and care.
We recall the words of Jesus
about the lilies, the birds, and our needs ....

Silence

Thank you, loving Maker, for meeting our needs.

We rejoice at the way in which
creation has the freedom to develop and change
reminding us of our own freedom and possibilities.
We recall the freedom Christ has won for us
and offer our free lives to you ....

Silence

Thank you, loving Maker, for giving us freedom.

> For the peace of lonely places;
> for the majesty of mountain and ocean;
> for the excitement of wind and storm;
> for the fascination of animals, great and small;
> for the glory of sunrise and sunset;
> for the beauty of flower and tree;
> for ...
> for your enjoyable creation;
> we thank you, loving Maker.

FAREWELL

Reading: Genesis 28.10-18

Companion God,
you travel with us on the journey of life,
matching your steps to ours.
This is an emotional time for us
as we say farewell to ... *(name/s).*
Our ways must part
as *he/she/they* travel on with you
in a different place.

Loving Parent God,
we praise and thank you for your promise
that you will never leave us.
Christ, who trod the path of humanity,
we praise and thank you for your promise
that you share our suffering and sorrow
and bring us to new life in you.
Spirit of God,
we praise and thank you for your promise
that you will guide, uphold and unite us.

We pray for ... *(name/s)*
as *he/she/they* leave us to go to ... *(place/situation),*
asking that *he/she/they* will feel you close to them
as you fulfil your promises.
(We pray especially for ...).
When we feel sad and bereft
help us to remember, with joy and gratitude,
all that we have shared together.
May we be constant in our prayer for *him/her/them,*
remembering that ties made in you
bind us together for ever.

Bless ... *(name/s)*, loving God,
as they travel on into *his/her/their* new life with you,
taking with *him/her/them* the insights and love
gained from being here.
May we all walk in peace and joy with you
all the days of our lives.

FELLOWSHIP MEETING

Reading: 1 John 4.7-12

We rejoice, God of our lives,
to meet together today:
    to share in friendship;
    to worship you;
    to learn something new.
Help us to be aware of your presence with us.

L: God our Friend, we pray:
R: Bind us together in your love.

Bless our fellowship meeting:
    be in the words we say
      to help us encourage one another;
    be in our thoughts
      to help us to listen and pray;
    be in our actions
      as we serve and help one another,
      reaching out with love.
Help us to welcome others and so welcome you.

L: God our Friend, we pray:
R: Bind us together in your love.

We pray for those of our fellowship
who cannot be with us;
for ... *(names and reasons)*
asking that ... *(appropriate requests).*
May they know of your presence with them
and of our thoughts and prayers for them.
May they know that we value and miss them.

L: God our Friend, we pray:
R: Bind us together in your love.

We pray for your world where so many are in need
    of friendship and understanding;
    of peace and the necessities for life.
We pray for ... *(situations in the news)*,
asking that ....
We remember that your Son, Jesus Christ,
died for all humankind.

L: God our Friend, we pray:
R: Bind us together in your love.

FLOWER FESTIVAL

Reading: Song of Solomon 2.10-13

Place a flower arrangement where everyone can look at it.

Let us gaze at the flowers:
>wonder at their colour and intricacy;
>appreciate their form and beauty;
>meditate on what they tell us
>of the beauty and generosity of God.

Silence

L: Loving God, for the gift of flowers:
R: We praise and thank you.

Let us gaze at the flowers:
>see how they brighten up the room;
>notice the water that keeps them alive;
>meditate on what they tell us
>of the joy and sufficiency of life in Christ.

Silence

L: Loving God, for the gift of flowers:
R: We praise and thank you.

Let us gaze at the flowers:
>look at how they have been arranged;
>observe how the arrangement enhances
>   their beauty;
>meditate on what they tell us
>of the Holy Spirit guiding our lives.

Silence

L: Loving God, for the gift of flowers:
R: We praise and thank you.

Beautiful God, we thank you for this Flower Festival.
We thank you for the flowers displayed here
and for the inspired skill of the flower arrangers.
We pray that the beauty and poetry of these flowers
may speak to those who come to see them
of your living presence in this world.

FUND-RAISING

Reading: 2 Corinthians 8.1-9

Ask those present to hold a coin in their hands.

Loving God,
you know what a big thing money is in our lives:
    if we have too little
        we are eaten up with worry;
    if we have plenty
        our consciences feel uneasy.

We have seen the harm that money can do:
    the exploitation of the vulnerable;
    the greed that destroys relationships;
    the thirty pieces of silver
        that paid for you to be betrayed.

But we also understand that the existence of money
is a necessary fact of our human life together.
We pray for your help, generous God,
so that we may use the gift of money responsibly,
treasuring it by dedicating it to you,
to be used for your loving purposes.

We have seen the good that money can do:
    the opening up of lives narrowed by poverty;
    the provision of shelter, medicine and schools;
    the resourcing of your church to offer its
    spiritual riches to the needy people it serves.

We pray for this fund-raising event
and for *the project we are looking to finance*; for ....

Give us the grace to draw closer to you
in our endeavour:
> in our contact with others, may we witness
> to the joy, love and meaning we find in our faith;
> in our working together may we treasure the
> riches of our shared friendship in you.

Saving God, bless all that we seek to do for you.
In the name of Love, accept our offering
of all that we have and do and are.

GUIDANCE

Reading: Psalm 16.7-11

God of the present moment,
we come to you in prayer
confident that you will hear and help us.

We need your help, loving God,
because there are decisions to be made
about ... *(situation)*
and we need guidance
to enable us to do things your way.

We ask that your Spirit will give us wisdom
to help us think clearly through the issues,
with minds unclouded by fear or negative thoughts.
Help us to listen carefully
so that we may hear your voice:
>   in the words spoken at our meeting;
>   in the words of those not here today;
>   in the words of Scripture
>   and the innermost thoughts of prayer.

May our decisions be shaped
by our faith in you
and by the hope we received
with the message of the good news.
May our decisions be shaped
by the love that called us into being
and desires the best for us all.

May the decisions we make
be a response worthy of you.
Give us vision, foresight and courage
and the grace to be flexible
in meeting changing needs and challenges.

We pray for those who will be affected by our
decisions, for ....
We seek your guidance that we may all
follow you along your loving way.

HOUSE GROUP

Reading: John 16.16-24

Place a large candle where everyone can see it, but light it later.

We spend a few moments in silence,
reminding ourselves that we have come here
to learn from God's word and one another
what it means to follow Christ.

Silence

God of our lives, we turn to you
with minds full of the thoughts of this day:
    of joyful, upsetting or disturbing news;
    of things to be done and words to be said.

Light the candle

Help us to focus on you, light of our lives,
as we bring these thoughts to you
and prepare to meet you in our discussion.

Silence

L: God, open our hearts and minds:
R: To understand your word.

We pray for the situations that are concerning us:
    for those we know ...;
    for your church ...;
    for this community ...;
    for your world, for ...;
    for ourselves.

Silence

We thank you that in Christ
you came to share humanity's concerns
and that you have a word of comfort and hope
for those who are suffering today.

L: God, open our hearts and minds:
R: To understand your word.

We offer you all we say and think
as we discuss ... *(subject)*
and seek to discover your truths.
We ask for insight and inspiration.
Help us to speak with clarity and sincerity
and to listen with enthusiasm and humility
so that we can hear you in one another.

L: God, open our hearts and minds:
R: To understand your word.

ILLNESS

Reading: Luke 4.38-40

God our Maker and our Minder,
we bring to you in prayer
those who are ill.

We have come to know you in Christ
as a God who longs
for human lives to be made whole;
we have come to know you as a saving God
to whom we can entrust those we love.

We pray for those with chronic long-term illnesses,
living with the frustrating limits of pain and fatigue,
unable to plan ahead or choose what they do.
We pray for ... *(name/s)*
and for their family/families, friends and carers ....
We ask that they may find you a companion
in their struggles,
> supporting and consoling them in their
> weakness,
> giving them hope and peace through their faith,
> calming their fears and heightening their joys.

L: In your loving mercy:
R: Hear our prayer.

We pray for people with life-threatening illnesses,
living with a dreadful uncertainty about their future
or with the likelihood that they are dying.
We pray for ... *(name/s)*
and for their family/families, friends and carers ....
We ask that they may feel you very close to them:
> comforting and supporting them with your love;
> encouraging them and strengthening them;
> calming their fears and heightening their joys.

L: In your loving mercy:
R: Hear our prayer.

We pray for all those we know who are unwell,
feeling poorly and finding daily life a struggle,
unable to do what they want or need to do;
We pray for ... *(names).*

L: In your loving mercy:
R: Hear our prayer.

Saving God, we entrust those who are ill
to your unfailing love.

NEW APPOINTMENT(S)
Reading: Matthew 4.18-22

Commissioning God,
from earliest times
you have called women and men
to serve your loving purposes
in special ways.
You ask us to be alert to your call,
ready to drop everything
to go and follow you.

We pray for those who,
obedient to your call,
are taking up new appointments.
We pray for ... *(name/s)*
in *her/his/their* new role/s as ....
We thank you for *her/his/their* commitment
to the gospel and the Church.

We ask that your Holy Spirit
may give *her/him/them* all that *s/he/they need*
to follow *her/his/their* calling;
may *s/he/they* be loving and wise,
steadfast and rich in faith.
Help us to support *her/him/them*
with our prayers and encouragement,
our understanding and our willingness
to give them the help *s/he/they* need.

We look forward, loving God,
to our future with you.
Help us to work and pray together
so that the world can see
the love, hope and joy we know
living by faith in you.

OFFERING PRAYERS

Reading: Mark 12.41-44

Loving God, there are many ways in which we can use
our money, energy and time;
our talents and our abilities to love;
but we offer them all to you,
asking you to use them to transform our world
into your kingdom of wholeness and peace.

We cannot earn your love, saving God,
as this money has been earned.
We cannot earn your love,
but we can thank you for giving it to us
by offering you everything we have and are.

God of never-ending love,
take this money and use it,
take our lives and use us,
for we owe every good thing we have to you.

The love of money is the cause of much evil
but money given away in love
can be the cause of much good.
Take our money, transforming God, and use it,
for we offer it in love.

How can we begrudge you anything, our God,
when we think of all you have given us
through the life, death and resurrection of Christ?
Take our willing gifts and use them
to share the good news of Jesus with humankind.

God, who rejoices in your people,
make us cheerful givers
of the things that we own
and the people we are.

OPENING OR DEDICATION of property etc.

Reading: Psalm 134

Let us joyfully bless our living God,
thankful for all that has brought us
to this special day in the life of our church,
the opening and/or dedication of the ....

We praise and thank you, loving God,
for being with us at every stage of this venture:
you were there at its conception,
    filling our minds with ideas,
    our prayers with a vision,
    our spirits with enthusiasm;
you were there in the planning,
    guiding our objectives,
    helping us to think clearly,
    opening our ears to one another;
you were there in the fund-raising,
    uniting us in our endeavours,
    keeping our eyes on the goal ahead,
    smiling when we enjoyed ourselves.

We praise and thank you, loving God,
for being with us every step of the way:
    calming our anxieties;
    lifting depressed spirits;
    encouraging us to carry on.

In gratitude for your faithfulness to us,
we dedicate this ... to you,
asking that you will use it, and us,
to further your loving purposes for humankind.
We still need your guidance for our lives,
your vision for our church,
your constant support in the midst of change,
if we are to continue serving you in your world.

May the joyful sense of achievement
that lights us up today
give us hope and energy for a future
lived to your glory.

OPENING SESSION of fellowship meeting etc.

Reading: 1 John 1.1-4

Creating God, who brought a new world into being,
we praise and thank you
because you continually open up our lives
to fresh discoveries of your glory and love.

L: God of new beginnings:
R: Thank you for this new session.

Word of God, who renews and restores us,
we praise and thank you
that in Christ you forgive our old lives of sin
and offer us a new start with you.

L: God of new beginnings:
R: Thank you for this new session.

Spirit of God, who sustains and refreshes us,
we praise and thank you
for the inspiration, love and encouragement
you give us through one another.

L: God of new beginnings:
R: Thank you for this new session.

We thank you for all the people
who give their time and thought
to make this meeting what it is, for ... *(names)*
and we thank you for all those
who come to speak, *inform or entertain us.*
Help us to support them
by our appreciation and with our prayers.

L: God of new beginnings:
R: Thank you for this new session.

We bring to you in prayer
those known to our meeting
who are sick, or sad, or anxious.
We pray for ... *(names),*
asking that they be upheld by knowing
your loving presence with them
and our care and prayer for them.

Help us, in this coming session,
to keep you always in mind,
so that our times together
may be blessed with love, joy and peace.

L: God of new beginnings:
R: Thank you for this new session.

OUTINGS

Reading: Psalm 8

We thank you, loving God,
that we find you in our church,
with us in the special holy moments,
reminding us to focus ourselves on you,
to open ourselves up to your word and Spirit
and to make worship the centre of our lives.

But when we leave the building behind
we find you with us everywhere,
reminding us that we are the children
of a God whose love, beauty and mystery
fills and lights up our whole universe.

Thank you for the outings we go on, loving God,
for the opportunities they give us to share together
in new experiences of your world,
to discover more about you in the things we see
and through our relationships with one another.

Help us to feel your presence with us
as we enjoy these times together:
inspire and teach us through what we see;
challenge us to value and care for your creation;
fill us with wonder, love and praise.

At the end of our *day* out
may we know the satisfaction of time well spent
with you and with one another.

May we feel
    peaceful and relaxed in our tiredness;
    full of happy memories of the day;
    and blessed by our shared experiences
    of faith and friendship.

OUTREACH

Reading: Colossians 4.2-6

Loving God, we thank you for the good news of Jesus
that has made our lives complete.
We thank you for breaking through
everything that divided us from you
and filling us with joy, hope and peace.

L: Saving God, speak through our words and our
     deeds:
**R: Proclaiming the good news of your
     undying love.**

Word of God, you want us
to tell everyone your good news;
to offer the Christian life, rich in meaning and love
to those dissatisfied by their lives
and those unaware of life's possibilities.

L: Saving God, speak through our words and our
     deeds:
**R: Proclaiming the good news of your
     undying love.**

Loving God, everywhere we look we see people
hungry for love,
people in need of faith in you and your goodness:
     those hurt or damaged by painful experiences;
     those not sure which way to turn.
Young and old, looking forward, looking back,
who all need to feel your loving hand upon their lives.

L: Saving God, speak through our words and our
     deeds:
**R: Proclaiming the good news of your
     undying love.**

Word of God, you call us
to share the good news of Jesus,
but sometimes we feel daunted by the task
and unsure that we are up to our calling.
We pray for the help of your Holy Spirit
to give us words that are 'gracious but not insipid'
and the wisdom and insight
to respond in the right way
to each person and every situation.

L: Saving God, speak through our words and our deeds:

R: Proclaiming the good news of your undying love.

We pray for the outreach of this church,
for ... *(any special project etc.).*
May we be an open-hearted community,
always ready to share our faith and friendship,
always ready to make the first move.

L: Saving God, speak through our words and our deeds:

R: Proclaiming the good news of your undying love.

SPEAKERS

Reading: Exodus 4.10-12

We thank you, God of our lives,
for every opportunity you give us
to discover more about our faith,
    about our world and
    about ourselves.

We thank you for this meeting,
for all that we enjoy about it.
We thank you for the worship we offer
    and the talks we receive
    and for our friendship together.

We thank you for those who come to speak to us;
    giving of their time to prepare
        and to be here;
    giving of themselves to us
        as they share their interests and their
        knowledge.

We thank you for their ability
to tell us of their interests and experiences
and to convey their knowledge
so that we can make it ours.

We pray for our speaker/s ... *(name/s)*
asking you to bless them and their words.
Help us to be good listeners,
receptive and responsive to what they say.

We pray for ... *any special concerns/involvement of
speaker*
asking that ...

L: In your love and mercy:
R: Hear our prayer.

You, loving God, are the Word of Life.
In Jesus we see the power of words
to teach and heal, to comfort and challenge.
May your Spirit give your Church
the words we should say
to our suffering and sorrowful world,
hungry for messages of hope and love.

TIME OF CRISIS 1 – concern for the future

Reading: Psalm 23

God our Shepherd,
we come to you in prayer feeling shaken and afraid
because of the future we see gaping before us.
We feel we are walking through the valley
of deepest darkness.
Everything in our lives is shifting and changing;
every belief and principle we cherish
is challenged or disrespected.
We cannot see the way ahead for us.
We do not know how to walk as your people
into the future.
Shepherd God, help us to see you walking
ahead of us.

L: Loving Shepherd, for your name's sake:
R: Guide us along the right path.

Christ the true Shepherd,
you were prepared to die for your sheep
and taught us not to fear death itself,
but the loss of the life of the soul.
We confess that we are afraid of a future
        where past beliefs and morals are dying out;
        where worship is no longer valued;
        and where people do not turn to you.
Christ our Saviour, show us what we need to let die
and what we should give our lives to defend.

L: Loving Shepherd, for your name's sake:
R: Guide us along the right path.

Holy Spirit,
we think how, on the day of Pentecost,
Christ's friends hid in the upper room,
grieving, afraid and uncertain;
and how you swept into their lives
filling them with joy, courage and purpose
as you guided them into a new and hopeful future.
Sometimes we feel like hiding away,
    guarding our religious treasures,
    preserving our past glories,
in a still but sterile atmosphere.
But we hear you calling us to live, not just exist.
Holy Spirit, blow into our prison of fear and doubt
and fill us with wisdom, confidence
and the power of love
for the living of future days.

L: Loving Shepherd, for your name's sake:
R: Guide us along the right path.

TIME OF CRISIS 2 – disagreement and conflict

Reading: Colossians 3.12-17

God of our lives,
we worship and adore you.
You were the starting point for everything that is
and you are the starting point for the way we live.
Everything we most treasure comes from you.

L: Loving God, bind us together:
R: Make us one in love.

We confess
that because our beliefs and our church
are so important to us
our feelings about them cut very deep,
leaving us vulnerable to infection by sin.
We confess the sins of:
> fear;
> arrogance;
> anger;
> intolerance
> and ....

Silence

We seek your loving forgiveness.

L: Loving God, bind us together:
R: Make us one in love.

We thank you
that in Christ you have offered us forgiveness
and a new way of living, as your children.
Help us to be more like him;
> full of compassion and kindness,
> of humility, gentleness and patience.
Like him, we want to be ready to give our very selves
out of love for our friends.

L: Loving God, bind us together:
R: Make us one in love.

Holy Spirit,
we ask you to breathe your healing peace
into all our disagreements,
    soothing our hurts,
    healing our broken relationships
    and calling us to a new
    and deeper understanding
    of the cost of discipleship.

L: Loving God, bind us together:
R: Make us one in love.

VOLUNTARY WORK

Reading: John 13.12-17

If members are willing, have a display about the voluntary work they do.

God our Maker and our Minder,
we praise and thank you
for giving us this world
to be our home
and our place of soul-making.
We praise and thank you
for making us in your own image
and for giving us one another
to love and be loved by,
so that our humanity may be made complete.

Servant Saviour,
we praise and thank you
for giving us yourself
to save humankind
and to offer us life in all its fullness.
We praise and thank you
for teaching us to serve you
by meeting the needs of our neighbours
and by loving other people
as we love ourselves.

Loving Spirit,
we praise and thank you
for living within us
and giving us strength and inspiration
for our Christian lives.
We praise and thank you
for your love that unites and heals,
guiding and motivating us
in our voluntary work for others.

We pray for those we know
who do voluntary work of any kind.
for ... *(names)* doing ... *(specify)*.
We thank you for all that they do and are
and pray that their work will be a blessing
both to those whom they seek to help
and to themselves.

God of joy, hope and peace, may your love shine
through everything we do and say.

WEDDING

Reading: 1 Corinthians 13.4-8a,13

> Flowers and music;
> lovely clothes;
> smiling families;
> sumptuous food.
God of joy and laughter,
these are some of the happy things that come to mind
when we hear that there is to be a wedding.

> Patience and kindness;
> humility and consideration;
> willingness to put another first;
> readiness to share troubles and fears.
God of love and life,
these are some of the qualities that come to mind
when we consider the deeper meaning of marriage.
These are the things for which we need to pray.

We bring to you in prayer ... *(names of those getting married)*
[and ... (names of any dependent children)]
We pray that this wedding may be for them
> a happy springboard into a new life together;
> a new life rich in love and opportunity
where they can grow and become
> the people you want them to be.
We pray for their families
that their love may also grow
as they become sources of friendship and support
for ... *(names)*
in happy times and in difficult times.

[We pray for any for whom the joy of this wedding
will be tinged with sorrow at the thought of past loss
or failure, asking that they may find comfort and
hope in this new start for ... *(names)*.]

Creator God, we thank you for the gift of human love
and especially the love
that comes to fulfilment in marriage.
We thank you for the joy and excitement
of falling in love
and for the security and friendship of married life.
We thank you for love that is never static and boring,
but grows and changes
with new discoveries and challenges.
We pray you will help us find this lasting and
maturing love
in our marriages, our families and our friendships,
and especially in our relationship with you.

WEEKEND TOGETHER

Reading: John 15.1-10

Lay out any plans, programmes, brochures etc.

God of community, we thank you for one another.
We thank you for calling us not only
as your individual disciples
but to be your church, feeding on you
and growing together
one in faith and love.

L: You are the vine:
R: And we are the branches.

We are looking forward to our weekend together.
We thank you for all the prayer and planning
that *has gone/is going* into its preparation.
We thank you that you *have been/are* present
in the planning, guiding, inspiring
and equipping those who are to lead.

L: You are the vine:
R: And we are the branches.

We remember how Jesus took the time
to walk, talk and eat with his disciples,
teaching them about the kingdom of heaven.
May we learn more about you
as we walk, talk and eat together
and share stories of your part in our lives.

L: You are the vine:
R: And we are the branches.

Help us to decide what we should take –
not only the practical necessities
but the questions to which we seek answers
and the right attitudes we need
to be nourished by this experience.

L: You are the vine:
R: And we are the branches.

Faithful God, make us brave and determined enough
to be truly open to all that is said and done:
    make us open to you;
    open to one another;
    open to discover more about ourselves.
Make us open to receive
all your messages of love and life.
May our times of worship
draw us closer to you and to one another
as we experience your love and joy and peace.

God, Father, Son and Holy Spirit,
bless our weekend together.

L: You are the vine:
R: And we are the branches.

WORLD CHURCH

Reading: Galatians 3.26-29

Creator God, we adore and praise you
for the beauty and diversity of your creation
which makes our eyes open wide in wonder
at the scale of your majesty and love.
We thank you that we can see
that your faithful people are to be found
in nearly every part of your world
and that your Church holds in its loving embrace
the children of so many lands, races and cultures.

L: God of the Church, may we be one
R: In Christ Jesus our Saviour.

Saving God, we confess to you
our narrow vision of your Church:
too often we take the word 'church' to mean
        our own congregation
        or our own denomination
        or the Christian community in our own country.
We do not appreciate the richness
of the World Church
or understand what we have to offer one another.
We are not open-handed in our giving
or our receiving.
Forgive us, for the sake of your Son
in whom we all become Church.

L: God of the Church, may we be one
R: In Christ Jesus our Saviour.

Spirit of God, open us up
to your moving in love through the Church,
so that we may receive your guidance
and your encouragement
and the gift of understanding
and trusting one another.

Help us, different as we are, to live as one body
so that the joys and pains of one
may be the joys and pains of all.
We pray for the Church in ....
We pray that your people may have
the wisdom to understand
the differing needs, cultures and traditions
of the many Christian communities in your world.
We pray that your people may have
the humility to listen
to the insights, discoveries
and prophetic utterances of others.
May we be full of love for you and for one another.

L: God of the Church, may we be one
R: In Christ Jesus our Saviour.

WORSHIP PREPARATION
Reading: 1 Corinthians 14.26

You, Creator God, love us and provide for us,
as a father cares for his children.
You give us all that we need,
and cherish us, even when we disobey you.
Creator God: we worship you.

Silence

You, Saving God, love us and rescue us,
as a shepherd seeks out his lost sheep.
You gave us your life itself to save us
from the consequences of our disobedience.
Saving God: we worship you.

Silence

You, Spirit of God, love us and inspire us,
as a refreshing shower brings life to the dry earth.
You nourish us with hope and courage, joy and peace
and transfigure our acts of worship.
Spirit of God: we worship you.

Silence

Loving God, may we feel and know you close to us
as we prepare worship for ....
We are thankful for the privilege of being entrusted
with leading your people as they worship,
and we are mindful of our responsibility, too.
We ask for your help that our worship may be
inspiring and uplifting;
reverent and relevant;
full of wonder and truth
and sensitive to the needs of the congregation.

We pray for our special cares and concerns
at this time:
for ... *(people)*
and for ... *(situations)*,
asking that you will heal, comfort and support us all
through the trying times in our lives.

Silence

As we prepare this act of worship,
help us not to be afraid to share our own ideas
and to be willing to accept the input of others.
We want to make something beautiful
to offer in love to you
who gave everything for us in Christ Jesus.

YOUNG PEOPLE'S WORK
Reading: Ecclesiastes 11.9-12.7

God of the old, middle-aged and young,
you must laugh to see
how generation after generation
the young are envied their youth
and advised to treasure it,
while the ways of 'young people today'
are fretted over.

    Fashions change;
    language mutates;
    morality fluctuates;
    money changes its value;
but the deepest needs of humankind
remain the same:
    the need to love and be loved;
    the need to be understood and valued;
    the need to find happiness and a purpose in life;
    the need to discover what is true and lasting.

Loving God, you can meet all these needs of ours
if we put our trust in you
and look to serve and meet you
in one another.

Whatever our age, life is never easy.
Whatever our age we face:
    problems;
    temptations;
    limitations
    and doubts about you and our Christian lives.
Whatever our age we know what it means
to be hurt and rejected, uncertain and afraid.

But we believe that you knew those feelings, too,
when you came in Jesus to share our human life
and to show us how to live
to get the best out of our time on earth.

May your Holy Spirit speak to us
through your word, people and prayer,
showing us the way we should go
if we are to follow Jesus
into a life of immeasurable love
and never-ending joy.

Index

Index